LAUNCHING
A STARTUP
IN THE DIGITAL AGE

Howard A. Tullman

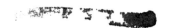

Published in the United States of America
For bulk orders, please contact info@blogintobook.com

Cover design portrait courtesy of Matthew Cherry
Perspiration Principles logo designed by James "Red" Schmitt
Special Thanks to Lakshmi Shenoy and Claudia Saric

To purchase all volumes of The Perspiration Principles, please visit:
BlogIntoBook.com/tullman/

ISBN: 9781619849846

DEDICATION

Sitting down every week to write something that will be meaningful and ideally of lasting value to others is a lot like setting out to start a new business. Sometimes there's a germ of an idea; sometimes it's an emotional reaction or other driver; or perhaps it's just a problem or situation that needs to be addressed. And occasionally you simply want to see things change and no one else is stepping up to the plate to make that happen.

You can't know how hard, long or costly (in many ways) the journey will be and there are no guarantees that anything good will ever come of your efforts, but you know for certain that nothing will ever happen if you don't get the process started and try. It's a lonely path and every bit of encouragement, assistance and support that you find along the way makes the job a little easier and slightly more likely to succeed.

I hope that these books will be my modest contribution to your success and to the well-worn and tattered bag of hopes and dreams which we call entrepreneurship.

CONTENTS

Part I

Fundraising in the Digital Age

Part II

Tools & Technology in the Digital Age

Part III

Mavens, Mentors and Masters of the Universe in the Digital Age

PART I

FUNDRAISING IN THE DIGITAL AGE

YOUR BUSINESS PLAN CAN BE YOUR BEST FRIEND OR YOUR WORST ENEMY

In the near future young entrepreneurs probably won't even prepare formal business plans because they take too much time and they're generally out of date immediately upon delivery. That's just a measure of how fast things are changing in today's hyper-competitive global marketplace.

In fact, personally, I'd rather be sent a demo URL and/or a prototype (minimum viable product) than a 50 page business plan (which I'm not gonna read in any case) because showing me what you've done beats telling me what you're gonna do by a country mile. If you've got it, flaunt it. If not, come back when you do.

Given the ease of entry into most new markets, the growth of lean start-ups, and the relatively insignificant costs of most underlying technologies, the basic threshold for your product or service to be taken seriously by investors, vendor/partners or even prospective key employees has been raised significantly. Talk and type are cheap – show me something concrete that differentiates your business from the 40 other wanna-bes in the same space who also have good ideas.

But, by the way, the fact that a good solid business plan is less critical to the funding process and to the outside world in general these days doesn't mean that it's not a crucial document for you and your business. One of the great lines in Hollywood about screenplays goes like this: "the screenplay isn't always the movie that gets made, but it's what gets the movie made". So you probably still need to go thru the drill to get some early funding, but it's ultimately how you use your plan in your business and with your team that's really critical.

Your plan's value will depend entirely on how you develop and employ it – it can be a roadmap or a roadblock. At any moment in time, your business plan reflects your best informed guess at the future – it's an educated guess and not the gospel. And it's going to change a million times as you progress because that's what building a business is really all about – it's evolving and advancing a central idea through continually changing circumstances.

You should use a business plan as a tool and a starting point to recognize and measure changes (so that you can react to them and adjust your actions accordingly) and not as an operating manual to run your business. It's not a cookbook that you follow blindly as if it were set in stone. There's a lot to be said for consistency in some cases, but trying to stick to a plan that was written in the past assumes that you've learned nothing in the ensuing time or from the unforeseen events that you've encountered. In fact, in times of rapid change, your past experience may be your worst enemy.

One of the greatest business shifts in recent times was quite a surprise to the public when it was announced. In March, 2012, the Encyclopedia Britannica announced that, after 244 years (but only 11 years after the founding of Wikipedia), it was discontinuing the publication of its print edition. At its peak, 120,000 hard-cover sets of the books were sold each year. But, no one at EB was really complaining because, and here's the shocker and the surprise, the print editions at the time of the announcement accounted for <u>LESS than 1%</u> of their revenue. And instead of those 120,000 physical sets, about 500,000 households were now paying an annual fee for an online subscription which represented about 15% of EB's revenue. And the lion's share of their revenue came from the migration to and the ongoing sale of curriculum products (math, science, English, etc.) to customers around the world. They had quietly and quite efficiently responded to the entry of aggressive new competition and the advent of new low-cost delivery systems by changing their entire centuries-old business in less than a decade to a new, agile player in the information marketplace rather than the book market.

Too many businesses run into serious problems because they waste time trying to make the circumstances they find themselves in fit their plan instead of changing the plan to adapt to and respond to the new conditions around them. You can't become so reliant on the numbers and assumptions in your plan that you lose sight of the facts on the ground and in the marketplace. The fact is that the longer you benchmark or measure your progress to an irrelevant or outdated standard, the more time you waste and the more ground you give up to the competition.

A model or plan doesn't necessarily get you to the truth – eventually the "math" stalls out and something more human and personal takes over – this is what makes the final difference between success and failure – call it intuition or faith or just the unstoppable courage of your convictions – the fact is that great entrepreneurs are pioneers and they embrace change so early in the process that their decisions will never be totally justifiable by the numbers. It's the art of drawing sufficient conclusions from insufficient premises.

MAKE ONLY THE RIGHT DEALS
AT THE RIGHT TIME

Next to having great parents, choosing smart partners and making the right deals at the right times (and stages) in a company's development are the most important external variables in the success of new businesses. Because, in the hyper-competitive and global market we live in, no one has the team, the resources and the reach to succeed by themselves. In these complex times, well-constructed partnerships, carefully-structured joint ventures, and timely endorsements and other kinds of supportive commitments are critical components in helping a start-up build its brand, credibility, momentum and customer base.

But too many young companies these days are falling into the trap of thinking that constant deal making is preferable to actually doing the hard work and the daily blocking-and-tackling of building their businesses. Doing deals for the sake of the deals or because it's exciting and different or because you're bored is one of the biggest time sinks and wastes of resources imaginable. And worse, it can create the false impression of real progress and growth when, in fact, all that's really going on is an excited and hyperactive chain of eager start-ups servicing each other with VC funny money and/or by burning through their scarce growth capital to do so. It's a little bit of dot. com déjà vu and my sense is that it's especially rampant in the area of social media "consulting" firms.

A quick credibility test that helps sort this stuff out is to simply check out a company's customer list and, if the average age of most of the business's customers is roughly 3 to 6 months older than the age of the company itself (if that) or, if half the "customers" are incubator/accelerator suite mates or other companies directed and/or controlled by common parties and investors, then you're looking at this year's edition of "smoke and mirrors". Steer clear of these guys.

But don't stop looking or thinking about what kinds of deals and partners make sense for your business which mainly depends on where you're at and where you want to go.

And keep in mind that your own time is scarce, expensive and valuable – you can't chase every rabbit or dance at every dance – have a few clear objectives; know where your business presently is; and know where you're headed. These basic filters will help you identify the realistic prospects and the wastes of time. I've always used 3 buckets to describe any business and to help me answer these questions.

A. Early - the business is emerging - deal objectives are:

   (i)   Help to build and expand the customer base
   (ii) Prove the underlying technology

B. Ongoing - the business is developing – deal objectives are:

   (i)   Manage and deepen relationships to "own" your customers
   (ii) Control and expand your platform
   (iii) Promote and encourage product and service expansion

C. Late - the business is maturing - deal objectives are:

   (i)   Expand and integrate third-party offerings and services
   (ii) Win with scale
   (iii) Attack or eliminate competitors and potential new entrants

Having done more deals in more businesses than I can even count, I've got a few simple rules that have saved me tons of money, helped me dodge more than a few bullets, and added a few years to my life. Take 'em for what they're worth, but don't forget them.

(1) Never deal with the monkey when the organ grinder is in the room.

If the guy who can say "yes" and/or sign the check isn't part of the discussion, you're wasting your time. Too many little monkeys and paper pushers can say "no", but only the real decision makers can green light a deal.

(2) When you settle for less than you deserve, you get less than you settled for.

By and large, deals don't get better or sweeter over time. It's critical to make the complete deal BEFORE you sign the final documents. If you don't like something about the deal at the outset or you're uncomfortable with the people or the process, it's only going to get worse with the passage of time. Ugly babies rarely become movie stars.

(3) The easier the deal is to get done, the harder it will be to implement.

Keep in mind that most of the value of a deal is realized or lost during the post-signing implementation phase of the deal. And don't confuse silence or good manners with acceptance or agreement. It's better to bag the deal than to bury fundamental issues or differences and leave them to blow up later. Only the lawyers and their litigators benefit from leaving critical questions unanswered.

(4) Short term deals make much more sense for start-ups.

Long duration deals are very seductive and very dangerous – too easy to enter and very hard to escape. Always leave yourself an exit plan and an "out" clause even if it's expensive. It's better to be soaked at a later date than to be stuck in a bad deal for what can seem like a lifetime to a start-up.

(5) Don't chase a deal that takes too long to get done.

Be prepared to walk away. Necessity never makes for a good deal. It's like being at the bus station. There's always another bus (just like there's always another deal) coming down the road in any direction you're interested in heading. And don't kill the messenger if a deal doesn't get done - think of these as mini-R&D projects – you want your people to keep looking and keep bringing opportunities to you. Don't chop their heads off if a deal blows up – it may be the best result for all concerned.

(6) Do small deals on a regular and recurring basis – go for singles, not home runs.

Small, quick, additive/incremental deals that don't burn up critical management time or resources and that reach a "go" or "no go" point quickly are the way to proceed.

Endorsements are a great example of small but very effective deals which can make a huge difference to the prospects of a young company. Very few people truly appreciate the value of endorsements until they don't have them and their competition does. This is especially true in brand-centric markets.

When I was just starting my computer game development company and wanted to create some educational games as well as movie games, I decided early on that some crucial product differentiation was going to be essential. I went after the Where's Waldo name because I thought it crossed over between entertainment and education and that for children's education games – Waldo was a very meaningful icon for the parents who were the real buyers.

And, I even got to say that I actually did know where Waldo was.

AVOID 90 DAY WONDERS

What kind of deal is a 90 Day Wonder. It's a transaction or an agreement where 90 days after you sign the papers, you wonder why you ever did the deal. And, <u>whichever</u> side of the table you're on – investor or entrepreneur - take it from me, you don't want to end up there – with a bucket full of regrets and egg all over your face. Even if Halloween's just around the corner.

There's a great old poker expression: "If you're in the game for 30 minutes and you don't know who the patsy is - you're the patsy." Needless to say, in any context, but especially when you're negotiating over money for a new business, nobody wants to be the patsy. And you can usually avoid it if you go into the negotiation process understanding even just a little about the needs of both parties; how those will change over time; and just how crazy most entrepreneurs get from time to time as their companies and their circumstances change and grow. Remember: as the Latin saying goes: "*finis origine pendent*" which means "the end depends on the beginning".

And keep in mind that I get to call entrepreneurs "crazy" because I "are" one. So please don't be offended. If you're a VC or other investor and I haven't previously offended you, it certainly isn't for any lack of effort on my part. I like to say that "asking an entrepreneur what he thinks about venture capitalists is like asking a dog how he feels about a fire hydrant". But I digress.

The fact is that, for many investors, each new deal and each new entrepreneur is a distinct set of experiences – so good, some not so much –

and it's an ongoing education for both sides of the equation that can be very instructive and also very painful. Education is expensive, no matter how you get it.

So here are eight different things that it's really critical to understand and keep in mind as you start down the road of working with entrepreneurs. The first 4 are pre-deal; the next 3 are during the deal; and the last is when the business is most likely in the toilet. I've used bullet points throughout (with a couple of exceptions) to save time and space:

1. <u>Be Careful Not to Starve the Baby</u>

Building new businesses may take less money today than it used to, but it still takes some basic amount of capital. In negotiating an initial deal, unfortunately both sides are perversely incented to starve the business. The entrepreneur wants to conserve his equity (you only give away your equity once) and to avoid early dilution at a low valuation. The investor wants to put as little capital at risk initially as possible although getting in early at a low valuation is an offset to this sentiment. The risk is that the business is undercapitalized from the outset and never has the resources necessary to get a serious start.

2. <u>Be Broader than the Boy Wonder</u>

It's the investor, not the entrepreneur, who has to make sure that whatever deal is made adequately provides for the entire management team (key players) and for players to be named at a later date. For the entrepreneur, very often, the business is a mission and a sacred crusade and he or she would basically work for free. But this isn't usually the case for most of the other senior people - at least not to the same extent – especially if they were lateral and/or later additions rather than co-founders or early members of the team. Because entrepreneurs are so intensely committed themselves, they very often fail to appreciate the differing levels of commitment that exist among the rest of the members of their team and they almost always fail to adequately provide for the rest of their team when they are dealing with the investors. It's very rarely an issue of selfishness and usually it's just the fact that they're so focused that they're oblivious.

3. <u>Be Sure to Ask the Hard Questions and Don't Kid Yourself</u>

Making an investment deal is very often a time-constrained process and, unlike a divorce proceeding where the lawyers on both sides are perfectly happy to bill their time and just wait until the parties calm down and get a little more rational before they try to get a deal done, in a typical business deal, everyone's in a hurry. And, because everyone wants to get to a deal, bad and ultimately unworkable agreements get made on a frighteningly frequent basis. Here are some of the things to watch out for:

Hard and time-consuming issues get papered over or buried to be resolved "later" by someone else (and sadly often through litigation) because no one wants to be the "bad" in someone else's day.

Otherwise smart and prudent people gloss over or entirely ignore their attorneys' advice on certain risks and with regard to undocumented or researched concerns (we regularly called our lawyers the Department of "NO") and focus only on the upside prospects of the deal.

In the interests of smooth sailing (and often with the excuse that "we have to live with these people after the deal is done"), even seasoned veterans will accept superficial assurances and smiles instead of concrete answers and go on to confuse good manners, pleasantries, and bad jokes with real agreement. The technical term we used for this phenomenon was "grin fucking" (where people are smiling through their teeth, but don't mean a thing they're saying) although there are a host of other equally descriptive and suggestive terms.

Too often, the negotiators push the problems forward and assume/delude themselves into believing that the fine details and rough edges will all be taken care of during the implementation phase of the transaction. All I can say about this is that – as a general rule in complex deals – (a) the easier the deal is to get done, the harder it will be to implement and (b) deals rarely, if ever, get better during implementation. Problems don't work themselves out or disappear – they fester and persist until someone takes responsibility for them and gets them resolved. Or, as the great playwright David Mamet once wrote: 'you can't polish a turd'.

Finally, instead of acknowledging and accepting that there are remaining open items and continuing uncertainties (that only time can resolve) and working together to construct metrics for determining the impact of possible outcomes as well as potential solutions to address changed economics, the parties engage in mutual fantasies and shake hands on deals which are full of holes and more porous than Swiss cheese.

AVOID 90 DAY WONDERS
– PART 2

As I said in the last chapter, 90 Day Wonders are transactions or agreements where 90 days after you sign the papers, you wonder why you ever did the deal. And, <u>whichever</u> side of the table you're on – investor or entrepreneur - take it from me, you don't want to end up there.

You can usually avoid this situation if you go into the negotiation process understanding even just a little about the needs of both parties; how those will change over time; and just how crazy most entrepreneurs get from time to time as their companies and their circumstances change and grow.

The fact is that, for many investors, each new deal and each new entrepreneur is a distinct set of experiences – some good, some not so much – and it's an ongoing education for both sides of the equation that can be very instructive and also very painful. Education is expensive, no matter how you get it.

One of the problems, however, from the investor side, is that very often you've got young, relatively green guys representing the money and, because they don't have a great deal of maturity or experience, they tend to fall back on a standard set of approaches, formulae, repeated mantras (that they seem to think are infallible expressions of long-settled wisdom) and other inflexible (and often inapplicable) views of the deal that basically have worked for them (or – at least – that they got away with in the past. And, often for worse, they try to jam every deal into the same cookie-cutter mold and approach.

Part of this is simple inexperience and a larger part is butt-covering where they figure that they can always say – in their defense if the deal structure ends up sucking – that this was the way they were told to do it in the past. Just as they say that no young MBA ever lost his job at a VC firm by saying "no" to a deal; there's also no place in the partnership (or anywhere else) for a whole lot of innovation, clever new solutions or risk-taking. Shutting up and doing it like it's always been done is the tried and true course. Gag me.

In any case, in the last chapter, I covered three major pre-deal concerns that are critical for all investors to keep in mind as they start down the road working with entrepreneurs. The next 4 issues (which are covered below) relate to considerations growing out of the ongoing deal negotiations. And the last section covers some very common comments and a bunch of rationalizations that customarily start to be heard with great frequency when the business is most likely in the toilet or on its way there.

I include these last quotes of both investors and entrepreneurs because they function very well as early (but sadly not early enough in most cases) warning signs that the deal is in real trouble.

1. <u>Beware of Hurt Feelings and Hidden Agendas</u>

Entrepreneurs are great rationalizers. Sometimes a modest delusion or a great rationalization is the only way you make it through the day when things are tough. As the old expression goes: if we knew how hard it was going to be and how long it was going to take; we would never have started on the journey in the first place. In start-ups, ignorance and lack of experience can sometimes be a competitive advantage – not knowing what you can or can't do opens up a far larger world of possibilities than settling for what's clearly doable and right in front of you.

In any case, in the context of negotiations, these traits play out in very specific and somewhat peculiar ways.

For example, to get a deal done, an entrepreneur will often accept (or really "settle for") terms and conditions that are unworkable and unrealistic just to get the deal done. He will sign up for the deal, but actually be crossing half his fingers and toes. Because entrepreneurs are eternal optimists (at least some of the time), they don't feel obliged to evaluate "either/or" equations because they think (but don't necessarily say) that they can eventually have it all or at least recoup what they are giving up in the short term. When this doesn't happen, you have one very unhappy camper.

Investors need to be careful that they never accept a commitment in words rather than in spirit. This is the same situation that all employers have when an employee asks for a raise and is turned down. You have to be sure that the employee didn't "quit without leaving". Happy to take a paycheck and do a half-assed job while looking for the next opportunity.

Another example is that entrepreneurs hate to lose control of any situation. But the very give and take that makes for successful negotiations and deals is a back and forth process of concessions and give-ups which can be viewed constructively or bitterly by the entrepreneur. Too tough or aggressive negotiations (even when the entrepreneur "agrees") can build up resentments that accumulate and that will ultimately find expression in harmful ways as time passes and the business rolls out. It's ALWAYS better for the parties to feel that both sides have left something on the table.

Finally, entrepreneurs are quick to feel victimized and taken advantage of and they fear getting screwed in a deal much more than any concern they may have about the business failing. Anger and paranoia are major emotional drivers and part of the personality of EVERY successful entrepreneur. Investors want to make sure that the underlying anger that's always there isn't directed toward them. One of the saddest things about even successful entrepreneurs is that – in retrospect – even when the deal has gone well, they still feel "cheated" late in the game because they are convinced that they gave up too much at the start. I don't know what else to say about this except to point out that mental health has never be a prerequisite for entrepreneurial success.

2. Back Off the Gas and Tap the Brakes

As the new business develops and expands, the interests of the investor and of the entrepreneur can easily diverge – especially if the deal has misaligned incentives which may be inherent in all deals rather than the fault of the parties. It's all about the relative perspectives of the parties.

Basically, the investor is always "on a clock" with at least one eye toward the door because his job is to ultimately harvest returns for his own funds or investors. More importantly, the investor knows that he will only have a small percentage of winners in his investment portfolio – some will be flat-out mistakes, some will be OK deals and some (maybe the worst outcome of all) will be the living dead – sideways deals that just hang on. So, when the investor sees a deal with real upside, he goes for the gas. He wants accelerated growth and he wants it sooner rather than later.

On the other hand, the seasoned entrepreneur certainly wants to expand his business, but he is usually focused on reaching profitability first and then growing from there. The main reason for this attitude is pretty obvious – the longer the business is losing money, the more likely the prospect that additional (dilutive) funding from the investor or others will be required. And, until the business is making a profit, other traditional and less costly means of financing growth simply aren't available. The second reason for the entrepreneur's attitude is that this is his business and he typically expects to be in it for a much longer time than the investor.

Bottom line - one is looking for a salable asset (near-term exit) and the other is looking for a self-sustaining and profitable business (long-term value).

3. "Business as Usual" Rarely is for the Entrepreneur

Every business encounters bumps in the road. They come with the territory and they are unavoidable. But, as inevitable problems arise, the older and more experienced investors react to the situations calmly and treat these things as "business as usual" problems to be dealt with rather than major catastrophes that are about to kill the company. In a real sense, "they've seen this movie before" and they've seen plenty of worse cases where some time, some planning and maybe a little luck got everyone through the storm in one piece. One of my favorite old-timers used to say that "things were hopeless, but not serious".

It's a completely different reality for the young entrepreneur who's going through the entire process often for the first time. To him or her, every problem is unique; they're all huge; and each one presents an existential threat to the business. While you might think this sounds a little extreme and over-wrought, it's completely real for the entrepreneur and it results in three material reactions which actually can have very serious consequences. In a sense, the business can get killed – not by the disease or problem – but by the reactions and the "cures".

In these cases, you can expect the following:

(1) The entrepreneur quickly concludes that the investors (because they aren't frantic) don't "care" or aren't interested in the business. This leads to ugly conversations and intemperate accusations which aren't helpful or constructive for anyone.

(2) The entrepreneur is irresistibly drawn to action – to doing something – pretty much anything – not because it's the right thing to do or a well-thought solution, but because the action itself is an antidote to the enormous anxiety that the entrepreneur is feeling. This leads to knee-jerk responses and wasteful actions which can usually be expected to do more harm than good. As Yogi Berra used to say, "We may be on the wrong road, but at least we're making good time."

(3) When you let everything become a crisis and be treated as an emergency, you lose control - not only of the agenda and of your scarce resources – but also of the ability to address and deal with the higher priority issues which are far more critical and which – if unattended to – can threaten the enterprise.

4. Better an Unwanted Guest than a Broken Business

Sometimes, like it or not, the investor needs to be a bit of "a bull in the china shop" and barge in even if he's not welcome. Denial is a powerful tool for entrepreneurs, but it can also be a big problem. It's not a process where you can ignore the facts and try to make the circumstances fit the plan – all the parties have got to be willing and open to changing the plan. By and large, if you don't think your business has any problems or room for improvement, then you probably have a big problem. And, in any case, I'd rather see a pivot than an empty pot.

It's been my experience that entrepreneurs pretty much never want to or know when to ask for help – a smart investor needs to invite himself to the party. Asking for help is embarrassing to these guys and most of them would rather die than die of embarrassment. The fact is that, in many cases, the growth rate of a start-up is directly proportional to the entrepreneur's tolerance for embarrassment. The thicker your skin – the further you'll go.

5. You've Got to Bite the Bullet When Things Go Bad

Words that you want to watch out for.

Investor's Perspective:

- This is Just One of Many Deals – I Need to Cut My Losses
- I Can't Afford the Opportunity Costs of Spending More Time
- Deals that Go Sideways are the Living Dead - Fail Fast and/or Pivot
- We've Got to Sell It to Somebody/Anybody
- It's not Actually My Money Anyway – "Out of Sight/Out of Mind"

Entrepreneur's Perspective:

- This is My Only Business – It's My Life and My Livelihood
- We Need to Keep Fighting the Good Fight – We Never Give Up
- We're Just "this/close" to Turning the Corner
- There's Always Another "Other" - Excuses or Explanations
- It's Just Money to You – It's a Crusade for Me

WHO'S YO MOMMA AND DOES SHE MATTER?

S ome people are just made to be entrepreneurs. It's genetic and they couldn't be anything but. Many of these guys knew early on that they couldn't ever work for someone else. They were just horrible employees. Others became entrepreneurs because they were influenced and pushed down the path by their circumstances, fate, and good (or bad) fortune. It also helps to have started a few businesses when you were very young. And it's definitely formative to have been fired – especially more than once – from a job you actually cared about. Finally, your family dynamics matter more and in more different ways than you think. Sometimes that's a good thing – others – not so much.

At the moment, I'm beginning to wonder whether, in addition to cheap technology and generally lower barriers to entry, a good part of the latest massive stream of new start-ups spreading all across the country isn't being generated at least in part by the last grand gestures of hundreds of helicopter parents (mostly Moms) in every city who still can't quite cut the post-college cord and who want to give their little boys and girls one last boost along the road to bountiful.

And so they provide comfort and continuing financial support for Junior's latest venture – regardless of the merits – and this spawns businesses that have no business being in business and a host of other problems – not the least of which is that the money that could be helping to build the right kinds of new businesses gets pissed away on feel-good fantasies funded by misplaced and misguided generosity – not to say – clueless charity.

I get that part of this situation is an age-old dilemma – whether parents should spend their time preparing their kids for the path and then set them off on their way or continue (for way too long) trying to prepare the path for their kids – and – very often – ending up just getting in the way. Too much support and ongoing financial participation (especially from friends and family) is always at best a mixed blessing for a new business. And that's really the much more important question at the heart of this whole thing – the latest frenetic burst of market madness – start-ups starting up with no rhyme or reason – based on ideas that are a dime a dozen – which employ lots of otherwise lost kids in made-up jobs – all of whom would be much better served getting any real job with an ongoing business where they might actually get their lives started and learn something.

Here's a hint. If your "job" has you and your friends living in someone else's fantasy funded by their friends and family (for as long as the money lasts), there's simply no good that can come of it. And you'll all eventually learn that – even in smart start-ups - money actually disappears much faster than it can be raised and secured and that - unless you can build a sustainable cash-neutral business that no longer requires regular dollar infusions from relatives or investors, you're just prolonging the business's inevitable demise.

Having too much or too easy funding doesn't usually help the growth process – it dulls the entrepreneur's edge – it hides the reality of what makes a business real (mainly paying customers and modest profits) – and it seems to me that it makes these kinds of businesses much less likely to succeed. If it ultimately doesn't matter to the powers that be (or the family) whether the business makes it or not because Mommy will always make sure her kids have a safety net, a soft landing and a place to stay, and everyone in the company knows that, the real question is whether this kind of non-critical consideration is likely to do the young business much more harm than good.

There's no question that most experienced entrepreneurs would tell you that being "comfortable" and secure in your shoes is a curse worse than almost any other when you're getting started. Working without a safety net is part of the process. You need to be a little scared, plenty hungry, and always wondering about making payroll and other ends meet. In addition, there are major personal and psychological issues in terms of the folks who are in the boat with the fortunate entrepreneur (and who have made their own sacrifices and commitments) when they realize that there aren't enough life vests and rafts to make sure that everyone has a happy ending. And finally, if you've always got one foot in and one foot out of the boat (and safe on shore), it's not the kind of true commitment that's going to inspire anyone.

Now before I start getting cards and letters from folks complaining that I'm picking on Moms, let me tell you exactly what the vast majority of successful entrepreneurs will say when you ask about their families and their relationship with their folks. First, they'd tell you that their parents were very often self-employed. Second, they'd tell you that they were the oldest or the only child. And finally, they'd say their Moms were spigots of unconditional love and that their relationship with their Dads wasn't comfortable or competitive (or even non-existent) – they'd say it was "strained" – whatever that means - and that's why the cash flow in these cases of (often covert) assistance comes overwhelmingly from Mom. Dads may help in other ways, but this kind of money comes from Mom.

So your Mom clearly does matter to your business, and surely parental support can be a plus in some cases, but that might not be good news if her "contributions" are actually holding the business back.

DEMO DAY DON'TS

I think most of the end-of-season Demo Days are officially over now - at least for a while. It's hard to be sure as the number of accelerators, incubators, and shared office facilities continues to race toward almost 200 different entities - just in the U.S. - and everyone else also wants in. Seems like someone's got something going somewhere every time you turn around. Still, having sat through half a dozen "days" in several cities in the last couple of months and watched more than 50 different pitches, I have a few suggestions for the teams and the teachers/mentors/coaches while we've got a bit of a breather.

I realize that it's easy to carp or complain from the cheap seats (and overall each year the players and the pitches are getting better and more mature), but since I've been there myself literally hundreds of times, I feel entitled to offer my impressions. You can take 'em or leave 'em, just don't ignore 'em until you've read 'em.

1. <u>One Size STILL Doesn't Fit All.</u>

Too many of the pitches were just too long. Early enthusiasm and energy turned into fatal fatigue when it felt like the last few minutes were just filler. Not every company or business needs ten minutes to tell a compelling tale. Say your piece - keep the emotional level high - and then sit down. Elaboration after a point is just mental pollution. Here's an old rule that has served me well over the years - "Just Because You Can Doesn't Mean You Should".

Sometimes I swear that it felt like even the guy (or girl) on the stage was just going through the motions. A separate, but related, issue is the risk of leaving your "A" game in the rehearsal room - too many rehearsals; too many coaches; and too many sleepless nights. Adrenaline will only take you so far and some of the presenters just seemed pooped to me.

2. Templates are Tiresome.

Your story and your style need to be front and center and everyone's story is different. The type of pitch (high energy, deep detail, quick quips, pretty pix, etc.) should depend completely on the specific message you're trying to send and the type of typical investor that you're targeting. Go with what makes sense for your story, not some set of boilerplate presentation slides where each team just fills in the blanks. Different strokes make sense for different folks.

Maybe your team is terrific and should be a major part of the pitch (after all investors mainly vote on the jockeys and not the horses), but the tenth time the audience sees the infamous smiling team slide, it's just tiresome and too much. Put the bios in a booklet or just bag the whole thing if your team isn't demonstrably a compelling competitive differentiator. You'll have plenty of time to introduce the team down the round.

And maybe it's just me, but I'm also pretty sick of meeting "Bob", the prototypical user or target customer, who has all the problems your product or service is going to solve. It's a painful and tired trope and it needs to be dumped from every demo as soon as possible.

3. Don't Let Your Dress Be A Distraction.

I think that - as a general rule - wearing your team's t-shirt may be the safest bet of all. Dressing up or down or too distinctly is risky. The last thing you want to happen as you walk on to the stage is to have anyone looking at you rather than listening to you. Crazy clothes, hiked-up heels, bushy beards, etc. all subtract substance, attention and focus from your story. It's just the way people are and it's not gonna change any time soon. Make your statement some other time and place.

I realize that there are plenty of smart and savvy people who choose to dress or wear their hair in a certain style, but in this narrow context, I think that a fashion faux pas can start you off with a crowd that wonders if you're serious and why would you want to start with that extra monkey on your back? This is a steep enough slope as it is – starting out in a rut of your own making – makes no sense. First impressions REALLY matter when you've only got a few minutes to make your points and your best case. And you don't get a second chance to make that first impression either – there are no "do-overs" on Demo Day.

I feel the same way about humor. Jokes are really hard to set up and pull off and they're risky. You just don't want to take the chance that your gag or stunt will fall flat and the crowd will start feeling sorry for you rather than swayed by you. They might still buy you a beer during the break, but they'll be a lot less likely to bet their bucks on your business if they think you're a clown. And a bad one at that.

4. <u>Case Studies Generally Suck</u>

Talking about your own results – user acquisition, revenue growth, major contracts, new strategic partners, etc. moves your story forward and makes a lot of sense. But trying to explain (as the clock keeps ticking) the details of a case study – even one with impressive results – is just a waste of too much precious time and – by and large – always a bad bet. You've got to set up the case; introduce the client and their problem; explain the context and the actions; and show the success – and all the while the audience is hearing the client's name (not yours) and you're talking about the client's business (not yours) and it's just too easy for everyone to get lost in the weeds. And frankly, they're not that interested in a one-off anything.

The depth of the discussion required to make a sensible explanation simply isn't worth the distraction. Just claim the results – "We saved these guys millions." – and move on. Details to follow. You can make the point that the product works without putting the audience to sleep.

5. <u>Funders are Fierce Followers</u>

I was amazed at how many companies said that they had raised X or Y dollars toward their goal, but didn't take the opportunity to say who their investors were. If your backers are willing, it's worth the time to tell us who are they. Brand name investors betting on your business sends a very clear and concise message to the rest of the crowd that they should get on board. The bigger and faster the bandwagon, the better the fund-raising results.

You should never forget that investors don't fear losing their money anywhere near as much as they fear being the only investor who does. Nobody today really wants to go it alone if they don't have to and, if things go bad, at least they'll have company in their misery.

MAKE SURE YOUR MODELS MATCH

In picking prospective partners or deciding which potential investors make the most sense for your business (assuming that you have the luxury of making such a choice), nothing matters more in the short run (and in the long run) than the proper alignment of the interests of the parties to the deal. Today, there's plenty of fast money to go around; lots of people it would be easy to live and work with; and plenty of players who, on paper, would make great partners. But if your dreams are different from theirs and your ultimate desires diverge, it's just a matter of time before the venture's wheels get wobbly and the vehicle runs off the road. And what's really amazing to me is how quickly the disconnects in these deals can appear and how obvious in retrospect the differences which drove the parties apart seem to any objective viewer from the outside.

I suppose though that, if the people on both sides of a deal want it to happen so badly, they're more than willing to ignore those ugly little facts and warning signs that don't fit conveniently into the big picture. Their hearts are probably in the right place, but their heads are stuck somewhere dark and entirely different. In this business, you've got to always remember that no deal is <u>much</u> better than a bad deal and that there's always another deal right around the corner.

And it's also crucial to appreciate that sometimes a deal can be critically important to one side (maybe even a life or death opportunity for a start-up) and, for the people on the other side, who are big, fat and happy, "corporate", and secure in their jobs; it's just another transaction – maybe even just a "take it or leave it" experiment – and basically nothing more than another day at the office rather than a make-or-break shot for a new business. And truthfully, whatever your business is, you don't want to be on the wrong side of this equation.

And we aren't talking about just amateurs here; these are some of the smartest guys in the room and in the media and entertainment businesses who are making these kinds of fundamental miscalculations. And this isn't a one-off case or an incidental "miss" where it's only a bad mistake or two – we're talking about quite a few. In fact, in the most recent YouTube example, there were hundreds of businesses and thousands of people and hundreds of millions of dollars involved and they still totally missed the boat. They went from being industry heroes ("content is king") to being non-entities and essentially homeless in less than a year. All because they had the wrong ducks in the wrong rows and no alignment.

So, when you see dozens and dozens of content deals all implode in a relatively short period of time, it's worth taking a closer look at what went so terribly wrong so quickly. After all, these weren't fake Wall Street junk securities or made-up collateralized mortgages – these were mostly deals that seemed pretty solid, but nonetheless went swiftly up in smoke. Not every one of them failed – but basically for its $300 plus million, YouTube ended up with a bag or two of beans and a couple of very expensive lessons.

Having been in the content creation business myself many times, I predicted the minute I heard the first announcement about these deals that the vast majority would fail because I thought that none of the "celebrity" or athlete creators appreciated how challenging it was going to be to try to create a constant stream of fresh and credible content for a 24/7 channel and how hard it is to keep up with the ravenous and constantly-changing demands of today's short attention span audiences.

My sense was that they thought they'd take YouTube's money (after all, who wouldn't take a million bucks with no real strings attached?) and then dump a bunch of pre-existing video material and other stuff they had stored or left over somewhere in the can into the new streaming services. Basically this looked to me like another generation of people trying to create just the latest pile of digital shovel ware – reusing old tired stuff - and trying to cram it into new delivery vehicles.

And while crappy content was undoubtedly a contributing factor to the failure and I was right about the results; I was basically wrong about the primary reasons that explain why this massive venture failed. The three main reasons things blew up were all about the alignment (or lack thereof) of the parties. It's hard to get to a happy ending when you start out headed in different directions. Same bed; separate dreams. And that's what happened here.

In July, 2012, YouTube announced that it was going to immediately spend $100 million to fund the development of 100 different web-based channels whose content would be developed and delivered by a diverse collection of producers, celebrities, entertainers, athletes, etc. – the vast majority of whom had never done anything like this before. This "Original Channels" initiative (eventually supported by another $200 million in YouTube marketing funds) was largely abandoned in less than a year and officially wiped off the map (shades of Stalin) a couple of months later at which point even a Google search couldn't find the original landing pages for the project.

So what went wrong? There were basically three critical miscalculations:

(1) <u>The parties' understandings of the scope of their respective commitments and of the duration of those commitments were misaligned.</u>

As obvious as it seems in retrospect, building and maintaining a media channel is an ongoing and constant process which not only never really ends, but which also requires continuous incremental investment – not simply for marketing – but for new production costs as well.

To the extent that the "producers" of these new channels thought in any detail about this situation, they were applying the traditional "network" model where a first season's "pilot" production is funded by the network and, if the show is successful, the producer looks to the network for additional funding to produce additional shows. Some of their confusion is completely understandable because both YouTube and others (like Netflix more recently) are completely comfortable calling themselves content networks even though it's not really clear (certainly in YouTube's case) that they understand what that means.

And, notwithstanding all the talk about next-gen networks, YouTube's perspective on the whole matter was completely different from that of the talent. They were applying the seed capital model and assumed that they would provide each channel with funds sufficient to launch and then it would be the responsibility of each channel's producers to obtain follow-on funding to the extent that the channel was gaining traction and initially successful.

In addition, as noted above, while this was serious business for the producers, it was pretty clearly just an experiment on YouTube's part and, in a fashion entirely consistent with their particular engineering mindset and analytical methodology, as soon as the data demonstrate that a venture's not viable, they turn off the spigot and move on to the next project.

What's the moral of this part of the story? You should never confuse a gift horse with a guarantee. And the "real" networks are not much different – they love ya to death until the day they don't and then they're gone.

(2) The "product" offerings and the prospective YouTube audiences for them were misunderstood and misaligned.

Not too long ago, and unrelated to the YouTube channel initiative, I had the chance to work with 4 of the leading and most popular "performers" on YouTube to produce some marketing videos for a new music-based video game. Each of these individuals/groups had spent several years developing a growing and loyal subscriber base for the karaoke music videos that they were creating (basically in their bedrooms) on a regular basis and they had hundreds of thousands of followers.

These 'performers" weren't well-known or media celebrities in any traditional sense, but they were pioneers in the emerging area of "camming" and they were all beginning to make an actual living doing their thing. They were creating personal and authentic connections with growable niche audiences and the "connections" they were building had as much and actually more to do with their personalities and patter than it did with the actual music they were making which was – after all – just their karaoke versions of pop songs.

What was very clear was that their audiences and followers (and, in fact, almost all of the steady YouTube video consumers) had absolutely no recurring interest in celebrity performers, traditional media stars or entertainers and jocks. Sure, they might drop in to watch one version of the new JT or JZ video on the day it was released, but essentially, if they were going to commit to anything on a continuing basis, it wasn't going to be some plastic performer that they knew was simply doing it for the money. They were looking for "real" people generating content that was not too far from material which they believed (rightly or wrongly) that they could produce themselves if they had the time, resources and inclination. Polished material, professional production values, synthesized sounds, etc. were all just a little too slick for their tastes.

So when YouTube launched the channel initiative with far more emphasis on the "hype" than the "heart" and somewhat cynically selected a bunch of performer/producers that they believed had significant niche followings which would follow them indiscriminately anywhere, the YouTube users basically weren't interested. Ultimately, the only channels that made it were the guys that had pre-existing channels and some decent traction before the new initiative ever launched.

What did they miss here? The real attraction, connection and engagement mechanism was not the songs or the sounds; it was the apparent accessibility of the talent and the shared social aspects of the group self-organizing around these performers as a connected community that was the underlying reason why large volumes of YouTube users were adopting and following each of them.

Sustainable YouTube success is predicated on nobodies developing significant niche audiences of true fans with shared ideas, values and perspectives and a strong sense of belonging to a community of their own making rather than fleeting and totally fickle followers of mass-market, made-for-the-media celebrities who have no authentic or actionable connection to anyone.

The lesson here is really about listening. There are plenty of ways and lots of tools to effectively listen to your customers and users today and to develop offerings consistent with their interests and appetites. Trying to create and launch new products and services in a vacuum and then trying to force-feed these with celebrity hook-ups and heavy marketing dollars on users who are already drowning in better choices is the worst kind of arrogance and stupidity.

(3) The timing and the scale of the channel development initiative and the fundamental adoption culture of the YouTube audiences were misaligned.

You would think that one thing which the guys from Google/YouTube would be aware of was the adoption/abandonment behavior of the active users on their sites. Another thing would be the law of averages and the unlikelihood that, out of 100 newly-created anythings, any more than a very few would ever be viable channels or worth watching. And a third thing would be that even the most committed and dedicated user/viewer has a finite amount of time to consume media and the average user couldn't possibly be expected to sample more than a few new channels in any reasonably short period of time. But notwithstanding all of these factors, these guys just went right ahead and basically launched everything at one time.

Consistent growth and sustained engagement on YouTube is absolutely a function of user acceptance and the passage of time. Audiences build slowly over many months and only if the content being offered maintains a high level of consistent quality. While it is true that certain individual videos (for reasons that no one can explain) go viral and, in a relatively short 0ime, can have millions of views, this has nothing to do with the idea that users would subscribe to or otherwise return regularly to a video channel to see updates and newly-added content without considerable marketing, substantial and highly-favorable word of mouth, aggressive sharing, etc.

But, instead of adopting some type of measured roll-out where small curated groups of additional channels (perhaps related in terms of subject matter) were added on a regular basis over several months, the YouTube channels initiative tried to blow out all of the new content (basically a "spray and pray" approach) and that's why essentially more than 90% of the channels failed to find any sizeable and sustainable audience.

What's the lesson here? Apart from the utter lack of awareness and respect for the way their own users operated and slowly accepted new material, and the sheer presumption that they either knew or could dictate what their users would like to see, they basically spent almost a year trying to push a rope. That is, trying to convince an over-served and essentially disinterested universe of viewers to change their basic consumption patterns overnight and to seek out and at least sample multiple instances of untested and unproven content.

There's only one explanation for why anyone would buy into this entire venture. It's the same classic observation made by William Goldman about Hollywood as far as what movies will sell and succeed. His conclusion was simplicity itself. He concluded that "nobody knows anything".

WHAT'S UP WITH DOCS?

As a former (or maybe I should say "reformed") lawyer, I understand all of the financial and other pressures on the legal profession these days and I sympathize with the guys who are just trying to make a living. But I'm also aware that, at the very same time we're trying to make it simple, faster and easier for startups to raise money (thru the JOBS Act among other initiatives), the lion's share of the lawyers working with new, early-stage businesses and entrepreneurs are still basically pretending that they need to redraft and reinvent the wheel every time they create a set of totally boilerplate, Seed or Series A investment documents and, worse yet, they're charging way too much for their services. I realize that it's getting harder (with more and more attorneys graduating every year) to find challenging and lucrative work, but that's no excuse for making work where it's not required.

And that's not even the end of the problem. Because many investment communities in a number of major cities and states are just beginning to fully embrace and encourage more centralized and concentrated efforts (as well as physical locations modeled after our 1871 start-up facility in Chicago) which are intended to channel, support and promote the growth and dramatic innovations inherent in entrepreneurial businesses, these areas lack the institutional knowledge, professional networks, and standard business practices (for better or for worse) which are one of the few charms and virtues of doing business with venture firms on either coast.

As a result, even after your new business has spent a small fortune (certainly in your eyes) on a set of basic corporate and investment documents, you now discover that you have the privilege of paying for an even more costly (and less beneficial or valuable) process where the competing lawyers on multiple sides of even the simplest investment seek (almost always at your total expense) to justify their own fees and their existences by engaging in stupid, irrelevant and time-consuming (and, oh yes, fee-generating) nit-picking and fly-specking of the same old documents that people (and businesses in exactly the same circumstances as yours) have successfully used without changing a single word or provision for many, many years. It's wasteful; it's offensive and presumptuous; and now is the time to put an end to it.

The truth is, as far as Seed round and even Series A investment documents go, there's just nothing new under the sun and the sooner we all agree (city by city, state by state, or whatever) to a standard, universal and stipulated set of basic documents which can be made available to all parties at a realistic (and modest) cost, the sooner we'll stop ripping off young, eager entrepreneurs and their backers and investors and let everyone get down to the real business of building their businesses. It's actually amazingly effective for an entrepreneur (regardless of the amount of leverage he has or lacks in a negotiation) to simply say to his counsel and to the other side that these are the documents that everyone he knows are using and that he's not prepared to start doctoring them up for anyone's benefit. And the really good news is that it's the truth and it's readily and immediately verifiable. What could be smarter, easier or more efficient? And why aren't we doing it nationwide?

So here are five simple steps for you to get the process started on the right foot regardless of where you're located and without respect to how many deals you've done before.

(1) Make Sure Your Lawyer Knows His Stuff

Every lawyer says he or she can do anything. They teach you to say that in law school because it's a good practice for getting hired. The truth is that doing deals is a specialized area and some attorneys in town and some firms focus on the work and do it better, faster and more regularly than many others. Even more importantly, they know all the other attorneys who also do deals for a living and they know the shortcuts, code words, standard provisions and restrictions, etc. because they all do it every day. And some of them can even help you get your funding by introducing you to their clients.

Go with a pro – not Joe who will try to learn the ropes on your time and on your dime.

(2) Ask Him (or Her) to Use the Standard Documents and Ask for a Flat Fee

Ask for the standard package of documents and for a fixed fee. Make it clear that your feelings won't be hurt if the actual forms and paperwork are done by an associate and not by the Big Guy himself which is what's going to happen in any event anyway. This saves everybody a lot of time and cuts down on the phone tag where you call the partner (who doesn't know anything about the status); he calls the associate (they both bill you for the call); and then generally a secretary calls you back with an update. Just send Sally the secretary some sweets and have her keep you in the loop.

(3) Read the Documents Yourself Until You Really Understand Them

You don't have to be a lawyer to understand the elements of a basic deal and shame on you if you're stupid enough to need to pay your lawyer to read these documents to you or for you. It's your business and your livelihood that's on the line – so spend the time and get smart at least once on the document package - because (God willing) you'll be seeing the same documents every time you do a new deal in the future. You don't have to be Perry Mason or Einstein to figure these things out and, frankly, if your lawyer isn't using a set of documents written in pretty plain English which just about anyone can understand (give or take a few special phrases which won't ever matter to you anyway), then he's not doing his job.

(4) Tell the Guys on the Other Side Exactly What You're Doing

Tell the investors exactly what you're doing and don't be ashamed of the fact that you're being smart and cheap at the same time. If they have any brains, they cut the same kind of package deal and reduced fee arrangements with the attorneys on their side a long time ago. And if they're smart investors, they understand that it's actually - at least in part - their money that you're spending on those legal fees rather than on marketing, product development or sales.

(5) Exchange and Sign the Papers – Get Your Money – Get Back to Business

Don't be a pig on valuation. Take whatever they're giving. Take the money and run before they change their minds. Get back to building your business. Thank me later.

FLAT IS THE NEW UP

I t's great to be living and working in Chicago. We're west of all the fear and frenzy that make New York so nutty and east of all the fame seekers and fruitcakes that make the Valley so frothy and volatile. In Chicago, we build businesses, not bubbles, and - in our city - bootstrapping is seen as a virtue to be proud of, not as a vice of the petite bourgeoisie.

So it was a welcome note of normalcy to hear Jon Medved (the founder and CEO of OurCrowd – the hottest equity crowding funding operation in the world – coming all the way from Israel to tell the assembled entrepreneurs (during his presentation at 1871) that "flat is the new up". Loosely translated, he meant that there's no shame in taking in additional capital and bolstering your war chest when the opportunity presents itself and when the investors are ready and willing regardless of whether you're also able to secure some immediate step-up in the putative value of your early-stage business.

It's important to always remember, as Jon also reminded the audience, that the only truly fatal mistake for a startup to make is to run out of cash. When you do that, they send you to the showers. Everything else in the life of your business is fixable. As I used to say, anything that you can fix with a check isn't a problem; it's just another choice. But when you run out of cash, they pretty much run you out of town.

Now you might say that Jon's a VC (and he is, but I think - in his heart - he's really more of an entrepreneur) and that it's in his interest to keep the valuations of the follow-on rounds of startup financing flat rather than constantly and automatically ticking up – especially those deals in which his fund has invested. And that would also be true. But that's not really the main idea or the overall message that I took away from his comment. I thought that there were some pretty valuable thoughts embedded in that simple descriptive phrase.

And I think that now's as good a time as any – maybe the best of times – to take a moment to reflect on where things stand and where we're headed in today's pretty bullish (at least for new businesses) investment environment. Because it's easy for bullish times to lead to bad behavior.

Let's start with a simple statement and a word of caution: the worst mistakes in business are made in good times, not in bad times. It's a remarkable fact of life that a small (and shrinking) bank account does a great deal to focus your attention on the things that are mission-critical and existential. You stop taking limos to the airport pretty quickly when you're starting to worry about next week's lunch money. I've been right there several times and, while it's good for your waistline, it's a lousy way to live.

But when funds are theoretically much easier to come by (at least in the current opinion of so many of the pundits and pontificators in the tech world) and the funds are being offered in ever-increasing amounts, it's a very attractive time to grab the gold and it's also pretty easy to lose your way and lose sight of the main and more important goals for your business. That's why an emphasis on the mainly artificial bogie of <u>interim</u> valuations (the math) is woefully misplaced when what only really matters is getting the investment (the money).

Until you sell your business or take it public and take a bunch of chips off the table, interim valuations are just so much chatter and cheap talk. Not worth the time to talk about and temporary fantasies at best. It's a lot like wetting your pants in a dark suit – it gives you a nice warm feeling for a moment; no one else really notices or cares; and you end up stinking up the place.

So when the opportunity presents itself to boost your bankroll; strike while the iron is hot and remember these three basic rules of early-stage fundraising:

(1) Getting money is just like eating appetizers.

You do it when they are being served. Don't be reticent or late to the buffet.

(2) Don't be a hog on valuation.

There are a million other deals competing for those same funds – many are just as attractive as yours and some will be much better-priced than yours. Pigs get fat; hogs get slaughtered. Just like on Wall Street. Easy money is what everyone <u>else</u> raises – getting yours will always be hard until it's done and in the bank.

(3) Take more money than you need because you <u>will</u> need it

– maybe for good reasons (radical growth or expansion) or for bad reasons (disappointing or delayed results) – but need it you will.

And ultimately, if you can't entirely resist being a bit of a hog on valuation; at least be the practical one just like in the storybooks. Take all the money you can get; say "thank you" (and not another word); and run like the wind.

MONEY DOESN'T MATTER ANYMORE

Today, for a startup, especially in the tech space, money just doesn't matter anymore. There's more money available today – even for mediocre stories and half-baked ideas - than anyone knows what to do with. And there doesn't appear to be any end in sight with more and more investors than ever before all frantically chasing the shiny new things and the few deals that they hope are really exceptional. As always, it's still a great big crapshoot in any event because (just like we say in the music business), it's easy to tell when someone's got a bad idea, but it's a lot harder to figure out the one-in-a-million deal that's gonna break through. So if you've got something special to sell and people are beating a path to your door, now's the time to let them in.

And there's another game-changing aspect of the money game which is equally important. In addition to having fairly painless, reasonably-priced and readily-available access to a great deal of cash, virtually every startup today actually needs millions of dollars <u>less</u> to get their businesses up and operating. In fact, they can even get themselves far enough along the way to hit a few major milestones on what we used to call "chump change". It's not like the good old days when capital was a central concern (and critical to your business's credibility and success) and you needed to raise a real war chest because – at least back then - you couldn't launch your company on sweat, smoke and mirrors with a few servers rented from AWS. But today, for better or for worse, you can pretty much get the ball rolling with some relatively modest funding and then you just have to start praying hard for both traction and momentum. However, it's still important to keep in mind that just because the barriers to entry are much lower; it doesn't mean that it's any easier to succeed. In fact, if you don't have <u>all</u> the tools you need; it's actually much harder to break through the noise, clutter and competition to get yourself and your business noticed.

So, if money isn't the be-all and end-all gating factor these days, what really does make the major difference in a startup's likelihood of success? I'd say that it all comes down to how you handle your talent. You can teach someone all about technology, but you can't teach talent. Talented and highly motivated people have always been and will always be the only, long-term, sustainable competitive advantage for a business and managing this particular resource is something that you need to do from the very first day of your business. In addition, we are starting to better understand that talent management is an ongoing, maybe every day, kind of job and not some kind of lay-away plan where once a year you try to make all the folks happy with raises or bonuses or options (or at least less unhappy) and then you generally try to forget about these things for the rest of the time or until something blows up in your face. We see this particular phenomena and the hyped-up emphasis on talent acquisition and accommodation in Major League Baseball right now where the balance of power (and compensation) has shifted dramatically from the on-field and dugout managers of the clubs who used to run the show to the corporate GMs who are the guys responsible for tracking down, tempting and securing the talent.

Now I realize that there are already plenty of treatises, textbooks (remember those?) and thoughtful articles out there about the need for (and the clever ways of) attracting, nurturing and retaining talent, but these things are generally written by people sitting on the sidelines like corporate managers, business school professors and HR professionals. Frankly, it takes a lot more talent, strength and energy to start, grow or change a company than it does to run one. And, as I like to say about picking surgeons if I'm having an operation: I want the guy who's done a hundred operations; not the guy who's watched a thousand. My life, and the world of startups in general, are not about "say", they're all about "do". So, I want to get down to brass tacks and into the trenches and talk about three critical things to keep in mind when you're dealing with the people who will make or break your business.

(1) Exceptional Talent is a Package Deal

A very important part of your job is to make room for people. Talent comes in strange and wonderful packages and – while we're happy to have the upsides – we are all too often not willing to understand that there are going to be trade-offs that come with the deal. You don't get to pick and choose and you've got to make sure that there's a place for everyone (including many who don't speak, act or look like you) in your business whether or not they believe that bathing is optional or prefer working all night long to showing up before the bell rings in the morning. Productivity is what you're looking for, not punctuality.

(2) Your Business is as Bad as Your Worst Employee

While it's still true that the best and most talented software engineers' contributions are a multiple of those made by the next group of smart programmers or designers; it turns out that there's a more important overall consideration. It turns out that the damage done by even a modestly underperforming employee is far more negative to the overall company efforts than the added benefit of those people punching above their weight. And tolerating mediocre performers is not only a horrible example for the rest of your folks; it's a contagious disease that can sink your ship. This means that another part of your job – not the easiest and certainly not the most popular – is to promptly and regularly get rid of the losers. And this means even the people who are trying the hardest. It's a sad thing to see people who have just enough talent to try, but not enough to succeed. Nonetheless, for your business to move forward, they need to move out and you have to be the agent of those changes. Waiting <u>never</u> helps in these cases. These situations don't fix themselves and I have found over the last 50 years that I have never fired someone too soon. Think about it and get busy.

(3) Even Your Superstars Need Support

I used to say that talent and hard work are no match for self-confidence, but over the years, I have discovered that every one of us has serious moments of self-doubt and crises of confidence. With extremely talented people, it's a special problem in their maturation and development. In their early years – whether it's in business or in baseball – the superstars can mainly get by on their sheer talent alone at least until the going gets really tough and the competition starts to even out the score. Then, at some point, they fail – in a project or in a pitch – it's inevitable and that's where you need to be standing by to help. Because it's only after you have failed – only once your raw skills and talent have let you down – that you realize that the really great talents are those people who combine their talents with thought and preparation – those who can add the power of discipline to their talent are the ones we come to call geniuses down the line. But this is a precarious juncture for these people who've never before known a rainy day or caught a bad break and, without some support – whether they ask for it or not – there's a risk that they can fall apart and never get their risk-taking confidence and their mojo back. If you've had it your own way for too long, you can come to believe (or at least convince yourself) that even luck is a talent. But it's not. At these times, if you want to hang on to these precious people, you need to be there to help.

BE A BETTER BOARD MEMBER
– BACK OFF

One of the recurring conversations I have with startup teams at 1871 is about their "bad" board members. I discount a fair amount of this talk because I have been on both sides of this particular table many times and I understand that most first-time entrepreneurs would be "pleased as punch" if their investors just sent over a bag of money, dropped by once a year for a nice meal, and waited patiently for the day they could help ring the bell at NASDAQ or just start clipping their coupons. More seasoned entrepreneurs understand that a strong, engaged, experienced and additive board is every bit as critical to the business's long-term success as any other part of the company's management team.

Nonetheless, I think this is an important issue as well as one which, for a lot of obvious reasons, is very hard for the entrepreneurs themselves to raise and discuss with the men and women on their boards. It also turns out that these issues are very hard conversations for the board members to have among themselves as well - even when they very clearly recognize the problems that may exist with certain directors.

The truth is that in many cases these days, you don't really get to pick and choose your fellow board members. So these concerns are just as much issues for the board members as they are for the entrepreneurs. The last thing that a new business needs is a situation where you have a bunch of micro-boards where certain board members communicate with other members of the board on sensitive issues, but not with all the members of the board. That leads to very mixed messages for the entrepreneur and a lot of hurt feelings – often, I have found, to be the result of mis-directed or inadvertently forwarded emails.

Also, more and more these days, you have very diverse boards (from an experience standpoint) and, in many cases, this situation puts very seasoned investors at the table with a bunch of angels (or industry-savvy "strategic" directors) who may have initially put their money in the deal (or their company's money in the deal), but who have very little to add as advisors going forward either because: (a) as angels, they lack any significant and useful business or investing experience; or (b) because as strategics, they often have no real "skin in the game" and tend to be reluctant to commit to much of anything in the way of hard decisions. I don't think you have to love your other board members (or even like them a great deal), but as a foundation for an effective board, you do need to have at least some basic respect for their opinions and expertise.

In other instances, the interests and agendas of the board members can radically diverge early on and make for some very stressful and difficult sessions where it's not always clear who is acting in the company's best interests and who is looking out for their own interests and agenda. I see this type of problem arise regularly in cases where the entrepreneur quickly falls out of love with certain investors either because: (a) they're too critical and over-involved at the outset (these kinds of businesses don't all happen to get built overnight) or (b) because the entrepreneur feels (often rightly so) that there were unkept promises and undelivered connections, relationships, introductions, customers, etc. which turned what looked like a promising connection into a bad arrangement from the entrepreneur's perspective. Sadly, in the constant frenzy of early stage fundraising, entrepreneurs make a lot of bad choices out of necessity and most often fail (with respect to board members) to heed that very important hiring advice about hiring slow and firing fast. Needless to say, it's very, very hard to ask someone to get off your board a few months after they've joined.

All of these considerations can be made better or worse by the behavior of the parties. I think we all know what the entrepreneurs can learn to do better, but I thought I would share a few of my observations regarding directors and also describe some of the behaviors and attitudes that seem to be at the center of these kinds of unfortunate situations. If the shoe fits, you know the rest.

Some successful entrepreneurs (even one-time wonders) can be great angel investors. Their decision speed; bias for action; appreciation of the ambiguities and uncertainties inherent in creating a brand-new business; and their commitment to seeing things continue to change for the better are all important advantages and reasons to have them as investors. But as board members, it can quickly become a very different story. Many of the very same skills, talents and attitudes that are benefits on the battlefield can be brutal in the board room. Among other things, they often suffer from "founderitis" – roughly described as "my way or the highway" and that just won't cut it at all in someone else's board room.

Great listening skills are an important part of being a board member and not something that entrepreneurs generally have in their bag of tricks at the outset. And I'm not sure that compromises, concessions and building consensus are even a part of the entrepreneurial DNA. So, as the CEO, you want to be careful before you invite too many bulls into your very fragile and young china shop. And as an entrepreneur acting as a director, it's a good idea to try to check your ego at the door.

Here are a few other tips from the trenches that I hope you'll also keep in mind.

(1) <u>Family</u>

We aren't yours. Just because your wife and kids don't listen to you at home doesn't mean you get to take it out on the guys you invested in. You're not our Dad and you're not Mr. Rogers. So spare us the homilies and the heart-to-hearts.

(2) <u>Flyovers</u>

Showing up is table stakes. Being prepared and focused is what we are looking for in a good board member. If your attention span is roughly akin to a Mexican jumping bean; try taking some Adderall and come back when you're calm. As far as drive-by mentors go; we say tell them to keep on drivin'.

(3) <u>Fables and Fantasies</u>

Just because it happened to you doesn't make it interesting or important to us or to the business. And just because things turned out well doesn't necessarily mean you had anything to do with it. Impress us with data; not dicta. Data always beat opinions.

(4) <u>Forget the Format</u>

The value and timeliness of the information is what matters; not the volume and weight of the board book. We'd rather have the right facts on a roll of toilet paper than a perfectly-bound book of boilerplate slides and a bunch of bullshit. Directors who are more concerned with form than substance tend to be the same guys who are more concerned with punctuality than productivity.

(5) <u>Focus on the Forest; Forget the Trees</u>

It might seem like the directors' job is to get into the weeds, but it's not. Their job is to set the broad strategic directions for the business and to hire and fire the CEO. The directors don't need to be minding everybody in the business's business; that's the CEO's and his team's job – not theirs. It's counter-productive, annoying and a great waste of time to try to end run the chain of command. It's there for a reason that smart directors understand and respect.

LEAVE A NIBBLE FOR NEXT TIME

Recently, I've been involved in a series of negotiations and discussions with a number of young entrepreneurs in and around 1871 (and elsewhere throughout the country) about a variety of topics regarding their businesses. Some of these conversations have been about the nature, usage and pricing of their products, services and content; some have related to the strength of their existing and emerging competition and the need for additional strategic partnerships; and many have been discussions about cash (or the impending lack thereof) and the pressing need for new rounds of financing.

On the last topic - new money - it seems clear to me that way too many of these guys (and girls) are getting miles ahead of themselves (and the actual results and progress of their businesses) and feverishly talking about raising big chunks of venture capital at very healthy and stepped-up valuations when they should be thinking about grabbing more angel money, generating some real revenue from actual customers, and figuring out how to get their businesses to break-even before their bankroll disappears. They're just in too much of a hurry to get everything done; they're losing sight of the need to make real connections with investors before you try to hit them over the head with your proposals; and they're trying to have it all in a heartbeat which almost never happens. Part of this is just that even the best fundraising process still inevitably takes some time - just like pregnancy. Sadly, nine women still can't have a baby in one month and you can't push a rope or an investor beyond reason and expect any real results.

To make things worse, I keep hearing about more and more expensive and time-wasting pilgrimages to the West Coast where these same people are meeting and pitching a dozen or more different VC firms and basically getting their heads and their porkpie hipster hats handed to them at every meeting because they're wasting everyone's time and - even in the Valley - they expect a little more than just pipe dreams and wild ass projections that grow to the sky. As they used to say about the Internet, and now they say about investment dollars, "the money's there all right; it's just not evenly distributed."

The fact is that there is plenty of capital everywhere these days (no need to drag yourself across the country in either direction), but there's no more money available for half-cooked concepts or half-baked businesses than there ever was. Your story and your numbers (and your valuation which is presumably based on them) still all need to make sense or you're just kidding yourself. Passion and extreme self-confidence can fill in some of the more glaring gaps, but there aren't too many smart investors around who've suddenly been hit with the stupid stick. I understand as well as anyone the pressure to make payroll, but you've got to be a little prudent about the process.

So, as you might imagine, these aren't easy chats to have with fired-up (and also very nervous) entrepreneurs and a bunch of these conversations have gotten pretty heated and intense. All of that's fine with me and pretty much business as usual and, frankly, it's even to be expected. I'm all for pushing the envelope, aggressive selling and persistence, but it helps some time to leaven the lectures and the "lessons" with at least a little patience and some perspective. In addition, a little listening to what people are consistently telling you doesn't hurt either. And just because someone else you heard about pulled a miracle off in record time with even less results than you have and found some whale of an investor almost overnight doesn't mean jack for your prospects.

But what I am really concerned about is that I'm seeing rampant examples of another epidemic of "egola" where the entrepreneurs are just so far out there with their demands and their expectations that they're becoming their own worst enemies. They're as bad as the Tea Party bozos and just as tone deaf and incapable of compromise or thinking about alternative paths, taking less money for the moment, cutting their burn rate so their runway extends, etc.

And, not surprisingly, when your "asks" are off the charts and astronomical compared to other folk's (especially prospective investors') views of the real picture, it makes it ultra easy to say a quick "no" and send you on your way. And this is exactly what is happening right now to companies which are full of good ideas and good people, but too full of themselves to understand and keep in mind the three most basic rules of negotiating good deals.

The first is the ancient business prophecy and truism that: what comes around goes around. Hopefully, if you're good and smart; this won't be your last rodeo or the last time you'll be in front of these very same investors (all of whom talk to each other regularly about the deals they're seeing) and it's really important for you to play the long game - pushing too hard and burning your bridges when you get turned down or over-reacting in any way is simply stupid. And coming to see these guys too early with too little is also a reflection on your judgment and your credibility that it will be hard to walk back and rebuild if you take your shot too soon and you're not prepared for the hard questions with concrete facts and good answers.

The second hoary axiom is that the best deals are those whereeveryone leaves a little bit on the table. I call this a "nibble for next time" and it lets everyone feel like a winner who got some of the things (but not everything) that were important to them. Everyone also feels a little pain, but they can go back to their boss or their team with a few scalps on their belts to show how well they did. And, most importantly, they feel that the other players were reasonable and that there are opportunities down the line to talk and deal again. That little nibble you left is a modest investment in the deal next time.

The third rule is that - at the end of the day - in every business people care much more about how their deal was negotiated and completed than they do about every little detail or talking point or even the final outcome. If your attitude going in is mature and healthy, you've got a good shot at getting a solid deal that makes sense for all concerned. But if it's all about winning and "your way or the highway" and it's not even enough that you get your way unless the other guys give in or give up; your deal's in trouble from the get-go.

This is because not only is implementing any deal at least as challenging and tough as getting the deal done and documented in the first place; successful implementation and integration will be a hundred times harder if the guys sitting across the table from you can't stand the sight of your face because you were a pig or an asshole during the negotiations. You can't burn down the village and then expect to be welcome at the native's weekly pig roast unless you're the pig on the spit. No one needs that kind of welcome - it's a lot like inviting a turkey to be your guest at Thanksgiving dinner.

So the lesson is that sticking to your guns and asking for all that you're entitled to is fine, but there's always a hard-to-read line past which you'll have gone too far. The only thing likely to bring you back is the good will (and a little slack and forgiveness) that you've accumulated throughout the process and the fact that you acted like a mensch from the beginning.

PART II

TOOLS & TECHNOLOGY IN THE DIGITAL AGE

TECHNOLOGY IS A TOOL, NOT A SOLUTION

I have consistently said (for longer than I care to remember) that, at least for me, there's a really simple test to evaluate the viability of an idea for a new B-to-B business. Does the proposed product or service save the end user time; does it save the customer or client money; or does it increase their productivity? If so, let's talk further. If not, take your plan and take a hike.

Now I understand that there are ideas for businesses that are intended to address other social objectives and that you can't measure those kinds of endeavors solely by their financial bottom line, but that's not what I'm talking about here. And frankly, those types of businesses are not representative of the vast majority of the proposals that I see every day. So, while there are clear exceptions to every set of rules, I'm sticking with my 3 simple questions until someone shows me a better approach.

And, of course, the ultimate dream is to find a business that does all of the above. It's not really as hard as it sounds especially today when new technologies are ripping through every old line traditional industry and turning things upside down. I see businesses every day that are disrupting the old ways of doing business simply by taking steps, obstacles and costs out of the old way that things have been done forever and dragging those businesses into the new world.

And what is so interesting to me is that the lion's share of the opportunities and new solutions (medical technologies are an exception) don't necessarily involve newly invented or untested technologies – they are nothing more than cases of smart people applying proven and industrial strength technologies to eliminate waste and inefficiencies and improve outcomes. This is the critical difference between invention and innovation. Innovation is smarter, faster, less expensive and less risky than trying to invent the next big thing from whole cloth. Good technology is necessary for great products and services, but it's not sufficient in itself to get the job done.

The new and inexpensive technologies which are now available pretty much everywhere are certainly enablers of the digital revolution (as is the rise of mobility and constant connectivity) and these tools make the process improvements and new solutions feasible and cost-effective, but it remains true that the real drivers of disruptive change are always the same: entrepreneurs (who probably didn't know what "couldn't" be done) and who look at things that everyone else has seen for years, but think something new and different and then go on to build something that changes the whole ball game.

Amazingly enough, once you have the cutting insight that changes everyone's perspective of whatever problem you're trying to solve, you discover that the "app" or the new technology is a conduit that is helpful in the process, but it's generally not the central reason for the appeal and attractiveness of the new approach. A good example is *Snapsheet* which is using mobile technologies (phones and cameras) to change the way that insurance adjusters do their work. Consumers simply use the *Snapsheet* app to take a series of photos of the damage to their car and upload it to *Snapsheet* where a room full of experienced adjusters immediately evaluates the damage and determines how the loss should be handled. Losses can be settled in hours rather than days or weeks. And that's just the beginning.

Snapsheet is one of those rare companies that are delivering a beneficial solution to auto insurance companies across all 3 of my test vectors. Time, money and productivity.

(1) <u>Save Me Time</u>

Claimants get settlements in hours. They don't have to waste time sitting around their house waiting for an adjuster to show up. The adjuster doesn't waste his time (and half a day) driving all over the city to look at a fender bender. In addition, using readily-available data, adjusters can instantly determine based on the age and mileage of the damaged vehicle whether any repair is appropriate or whether they should just "total" the car and write a check on the spot.

(2) <u>Save Me Money</u>

Insurers save boatloads of money avoiding the costs of providing rental cars for their insureds. Transportation and fuels costs shrink dramatically. Faster settlements have less unhappy parties and significantly fewer supplementary payments.

(3) <u>Increase My Productivity</u>

Adjusters can process far more claims every day because they aren't wasting travel time and gas on useless trips. In addition, they're sitting in a room surrounded by other expert adjusters instead of being The Lone Ranger standing out in some cornfield or driveway trying to write an estimate. Faster, better, more accurate and fully documented transactions mean happier insureds and employees as well.

But the thing that is so striking is that the major benefits from using *Snapsheet* don't really arise from the "app" or the underlying technology – any mobile device that can capture and send images could get the job done – the real value arises from smart (and now obvious) improvements in the efficiency of the adjusting process. This is why the best businesses don't lead with their technology – they lead with solution selling addressed to known and obvious problems.

WHY DIGITAL WINS

I have to laugh and just shake my head when people tell me that they are working on the digital strategy for their business or reluctantly ask me to help them figure out what they should be doing about social media as if it's a new form of head lice or psoriasis or something equally disgusting, contagious and unavoidable. It's a little like saying that you've decided you're going to spend a little time each day breathing – even though you're pretty busy with a bunch of other commitments – because it seems like the smart thing to do.

Digital technologies and social media channels and the new degrees and depth of "connection" that they enable are so mission-critical these days and so pervade every aspect of what we need to be doing in our lives and companies – as every business in the world migrates rapidly from analog anything to digital everything – that the incorporation of these powerful tools and technologies isn't an option or a choice, they are inevitable additions to your arsenal and, frankly, the sooner the better. I see the two alternative paths as very binary – you can engage or you can be extinct. Change and grow or die – pretty stark choices. You can face the facts or you can be like that lonesome old fax machine sitting in the corner just dreading the day when it will finally be unplugged and trashed.

This is a major topic which is well-suited for a series of columns, but, for the moment, I just want to give you a short list of the 5 major dimensions of enablement which digital is bringing to the game. If you ask yourself what you are doing or about to do in your business to take advantage of these new resources, tools, technologies, channels and perspectives which are now available basically because of the digital datafication of everything, you'll get a head start on your peers and competitors. It's not an easy process or a short path, but it's already well underway and you need to get with the program or get left behind. It's always the same story: you can make the dust or you can eat someone else's dust.

One crucial aspect of this ongoing and highly-disruptive transformation which the mass media really doesn't seem to appreciate is that the most critical attribute of the Internet is NOT its immediacy or its low cost; it is the heightened direct access to identified individuals, the ability to accurately measure and react to their ongoing engagement in real time, and the media spend direction and accountability that it enables.

Here are the 5 vital vectors:

(1) <u>Superior Customer Targeting and Offer Optimization</u>

I've talked before about hyper-personalization (customer demographics) which morphed quickly into determining and tracking interests and attitudes (customer preferences and desires) and now we're moving forward again to anticipatory actions which let us drive and leverage future customer behaviors. This is a page right out of the canon of Steve Jobs who basically said that consumers don't know what they want until we create it and show it to them. Or as Henry Ford might have said about consumer demand for the Model T: If I had asked people at the time what they wanted, they would have said they needed faster horses, not automobiles.

(2) <u>New Levels of Analytics & Insights Based on Speed & Scale</u>

Size is nice, but in today's world, speed is what kills. It's not the big guys who are moving the needle today; it's the fast and responsive guys. Everything we're doing today in marketing is time-compressed and the rate of required change continues to accelerate. You'll never see smart marketers buying 12 week campaigns any longer and then sitting back and hoping things work out well. We have tools to see how things are trending in our campaigns on a minute-to-minute basis and today that's the standard for reacting to those behaviors as well. We're not talking about an A/B testing world any more. We're talking about A to Z systems that can launch 20 alternative offers to a small (and inexpensive, but representative) segment of a target list; collect and collate the responses in real time (minutes rather than months); prioritize the winning pitches and kill off the losers and then launch the winners against the larger lists and continue this iterative process all day long. No one said it was gonna be easy – just essential. And the ante just keeps getting upped.

If you haven't seen and started to use GOOGLE Product Listing Ads (PLAs), you're late. But what's most important is to understand – not how much more appealing a GOOGLE search response is which features multiple responsive product images and pricing from local merchants – you need to appreciate how much more work this represents for each local merchant. Every product has to be imaged, catalogued, loaded and priced (realistically, the pricing almost needs to be dynamic for your particular offerings to remain competitive) and the whole thing needs to be actively managed and updated constantly. It's a whole every day job just to stay in the game and increasingly it's going to have to be machine-driven and informed – much like programmed stock trading. But who's going to create and supply these kinds of tools for SMBs to permit them to remain competitive in these new, high-speed marketplaces? I see this whole area as just another amazing set of opportunities for entrepreneurs. But even if you're not building the new tools for the rest of us, you'd better be doing something in your business to respond.

(3) Ability to Change Consumer Behaviors in Real Time

If you're always reacting (regardless of how quickly) to the behavior of the consumers you're trying to reach, in today's world of high-velocity computing, you'll always be behind the curve and behind your competition because the game is now to get ahead of the consumer and to "know before they go" so that you can be there when they arrive. Sites like www.chango. com offer these kinds of tools for smart marketers with response and reaction times in the area of 10 milliseconds – faster than a webpage can load. As you can imagine, if I'm taking search results (what you found) and I'm trying to launch offers to you in response to those searches, I'm going to <u>always</u> lose out to the competitors whose tools and technologies enable them to determine what I'm looking for and present me with those choices rather than waiting for me to ask or find the answers on my own. It's a world moving from diagnostics (historical analysis) to prognostics (anticipation and prediction) and you need to get your business on the bus or you'll be left behind.

(4) <u>Two-Way Channels for Ongoing Consumer Conversations</u>

The ability to have ongoing, long-term, unmediated and bi-directional conversations with our customers on a massive scale provides us with the tools and channels we need to increase the lifetime value of each customer (LCV). Nothing is more directly connected to profitability than growing your share of each of your customers' spend and improving your retention of those customers. You now have the ability to determine - not simply whether your customers are seeing or hearing your messages, but whether they are listening to them and responding to them in meaningful ways. We've moved from a broadcast world (call it "spray and pray") to improved and more targeted unilateral communications and now we're moving forward again to two-way talks and credible conversations.

(5) <u>Concrete and Readily Available Metrics - CAC, CSI, CRM</u>

Data is the Oil of the Digital Age. If you don't already understand how critical access to and the constant measurement of the data which drives your business has become to your survival (not simply your success), there's not much I can add to the discussion. As Louis Armstrong used to say: "If you have to ask what jazz is, you'll never know".

FIND ME A FLYWHEEL TO MAKE
ME A FORTUNE

I've seen the future and it's a flywheel. Not a physical flywheel, but a system that – for all intents and purposes – is actually its more expansive and digital equivalent. A system that replaces the momentum which a flywheel creates and gathers as it spins and accelerates with the expansive digital power which we have come to call the "network effect". Actually, my favorite flywheel these days isn't a physical or digital object at all – it's a relatively new, second-generation (or maybe a third generation) ad tech startup business based in New York which is called *Simple Reach* (www. simplereach.com) and which has built tools and a measurement/content distribution platform that permits publishers and brands to make much more effective and intelligent use of all of the branded and sponsored content they are creating to help them burnish their brands and better connect at a higher level with their customers.

The network effect (which was first formulated by George Gilder and is now generally known as Metcalfe's Law) is basically a description of the expanding value of a communications network as it adds additional nodes or links. The rate of growth in the intrinsic value of the network is not linear, but exponential and multiplies ever faster as the network expands. What *Simple Reach* has done is create an enterprise model where its customers themselves (as well as interested third parties who may be prospective customers) increasingly help build *SR*'s business and grow its user and customer base (without any direct compensation) mainly because it serves their own selfish and competitive interests to do so. There's no more authentic and convincing promoter and marketer for your business than a satisfied customer who makes it his or her business to invite more people to the party. That's the flywheel in action.

Why do they do this?

First because it dramatically increases the value of the *SR* tools and services for each of them in their own businesses. You can never go wrong counting on smart business people to act in their own self-interest. From the brand's standpoint, each new publisher added to the *SR* reporting network increases the brand's ability to more fully measure – in a unified and standardized manner – the value and impact of its spending on a given campaign. From the publisher's standpoint, each new brand added to the program (by the publisher or independently by *SR*) which then has the ability to extend its ongoing and new campaigns and its marketing spend to that publisher's channels creates more revenue opportunities and more of a one-stop solution set for the publisher.

And second, because the publishers (and frankly the agencies as well) really have no choice but to adopt such a system because their own customers are starting to demand that they use the *SR* methodology and provide them with the results which they can then readily fold into their own analysis. Sometimes a given brand will have learned about the *Simple Reach* service from a different use case with a different publisher (or obviously from *SR* itself – although they do very little sales or marketing right now – relying mainly on word-of-mouth and cross-referrals) and then – in discussions with other publishers, the brand will expect and often specify this type of data and reporting and make it clear that – if such support is not available – it will be pleased to take its business elsewhere. Frankly, no publisher today can afford to be without these kinds of offerings which are really the newest and most powerful windows to the digital world.

And finally, because, if the middle men (publishers or agencies) don't provide these services to their customers (the brands), the customers will go right around them directly to *Simple Reach* and sign up for the services. And, as it happens, that's already beginning to happen as the ultimate brand customers start to understand that they need these tools for all their marketing channels and not simply for the initial channel (or agency or publisher) which may have brought the *SR* service to their attention. Frankly, the brands already see themselves more and more as content publishers anyway and so it's a simple step (no pun intended) to contract directly for these kinds of resources – especially when – as noted above - they provide constantly more efficient one-stop shopping and integrated surveillance and tracking dashboards.

This is the kind of growth engine that you want to hang your hat on and then hold on tight for the rapid ride. And it's the kind that's very hard to come by and, as often as not, may end up flying off the track and throwing everyone for a loss. But if you find the right engine in the right marketplace and environment and your guy is the first player there, then the extent of the potential upside is hard to imagine.

It's not simply that (a) pervasive and truly additive platforms – once in place – are almost impossible to dislodge and (b) that increasingly technology spaces are becoming more and more "winner take all" plays; it's that the momentum and the earning potential accelerates at such an overwhelmingly rapid pace that even the biggest players can't respond quickly enough to the new competitive threat or use their size and resources effectively to offset the early advantages of the growing cash cushion of the first mover.

Especially in the case of a new business, that cash cushion provides several layers of comfort and security. First, management can focus on the business, not on what often – in new growing businesses - feels like perpetual fundraising. Second, early mistakes are less likely to threaten the business's existence since the business can pivot if necessary without payroll becoming a problem. Third, the customers are comforted by the bankroll and much less concerned about betting their business on the newest kid in town. Fourth, the company can afford to support simultaneous pilots and trials for far more customers than most startups. And finally, there's very little pressure on the pricing of the business's services since the company doesn't have to engage in price cutting in order to win new accounts.

But there's an even more powerful factor at work in cases like this and it's the "lock-in" investment (not in terms of dollars, but in terms of tangible business benefits) which creates powerful barriers and overwhelming switching costs even for those clients and customers which are willing to consider any kind of shift or movement. Both of these considerations are not matters of dollars and sense; they are concerns that anyone attempting to switch and losing even a moment's time or presence in these fiercely competitive marketplaces would be irreparably damaged and disadvantaged to such an extent that any such considerations would never be worth the risk.

As a result, flywheel businesses enjoy another interesting benefit – the customers seek out and readily agree to multi-year contracts - which is somewhat counter-intuitive when you are dealing with new, young companies until you realize just how quickly these kinds of new data services become mission-critical to the customers and just how addictive and additive they can be. The customers (who ordinarily would be reluctant to make longer-term commitments to a startup) quickly start to attempt to sign multi-year agreements for two reasons: (1) they become concerned about the startup's overall capacity to meet the growing demand for its offerings and they want to be sure that their own needs will continue to be met; and (b) as they incorporate the new company's products and services into their own businesses, they want to be sure that the company sticks around and stays in business.

As long as the startup retains the ability over time to continue to raise its prices and otherwise adapt and improve its products and services, this is nothing but great news for the new business because it creates unexpected levels of stability, predictable future revenue streams, and assurances that the company's future is sufficiently secure that it can make appropriate growth plans and also attract first-class talent to what would otherwise appear to be a far riskier opportunity.

So what does all this say about the future of content marketing (which continues to grow like crazy as the big brand advertisers try to create viable and continuing substantive/emotional connections with their customers) and what do you need to be thinking about for your business as you try to determine how to most profitably spend your digital marketing resources?

First, it's important to understand that we are moving into the second generation of the digital marketing revolution. If the first generation was the brute force ability to get your material (content) and your associated messages out and in front of the digital consumer (on every device), the second generation is all about tracking and measuring the efficacy and amplification of those efforts and getting better at getting it out there all the time. It's no longer about tonnage – it's all about transparency and touching the right targets at the right time in order to deliver the appropriate information and incentives to them.

Second, especially in the media/publishing marketplace, accountability is now the be-all and the end-all. No one takes your word for anything these days – no matter how much wine you pour down them - it's a "show me or see ya" world and the winners are the ones with the documentation and the ammunition to make their cases. If you can't convincingly connect spend to traffic to engagement (and organic sharing) and ultimately to conversions and concrete results, you really can't compete for much longer in this space.

We know most of these initiatives won't work, but we need to know which are working and which aren't as soon as possible so we can tactically adjust the aggregate dollar spend in order to optimize our dollars and our results. The old idea that you would simply "set it and forget it"; spend ratably the same amounts across various campaign channels; and sit back and wait for the results might have been the only way to go in the old days before we had real time responses and metrics, but it's a lazy and stupid strategy today.

And even discussing the best post-campaign documentation feels a lot like too little and too late because it's fundamentally about after-the-fact analysis and not utilizing ongoing actionable insights. The best players are focused on prognosis (prediction and real-time adjustment) rather than diagnosis which is basically all about looking backwards to see what worked. You want to be able to shift the sands under the consumers' feet and up the ante when you see where it makes sense to increase the spending behind already successful sharing in order to press your bet, amplify the impact, and increase the return on your initial investment in the development, creation and delivery of that content.

And so, in this newest media world, the real winners will be the ones who can not only help their clients track and measure effectiveness in real-time, but whose tools permit them to immediately take the next and most critical actions to accelerate and double down on what is working before these fleeting opportunities pass them by. It's an old venture capital rule of thumb – you feed your winners and you starve your losers. And that's where the guys at *Simple Reach* really come into their own as their rapid growth and multi-line expansion are showing. As I always say, you want to be there when the customer wants to buy and *Simple Reach* helps its clients track and get the right messages in front of the right customers in order to reach them at the right moment – when they are receptive and ready to buy.

It's that simple (no pun intended), but it's not easy and these guys are simply crushing it.

LOOK FOR LEAPFROGGING, NOT LINEAR, ADVANCES

Too much of our planning for growth these days is predicated on incremental improvements, brand extensions, product re-sizing, territorial expansions and the like. These are attempts to capture market share available in readily-apparent adjacencies rather than through undertaking new journeys and adventures and they're generally safe and sound bets for big companies. One problem with this approach is that these are paths and choices that are demonstrably evolutionary rather than revolutionary – they're great add-ons, but rarely will they generate needle-moving numbers. Sure bets guarantee small margins. The standard "no one ever got fired" process is all about taking carefully-qualified steps forward instead of making quantum leaps.

But it's becoming increasingly clear that this heads-down, "grind it out" approach (which might have been entirely prudent and reasonable in less flush or chaotic times) keeps many of us from seeing and seizing certain kinds of disruptive and game-changing opportunities which are being enabled today primarily by the rapid spread and availability of new low-cost technologies and by the dual explosion of ubiquitous mobility and connectivity. If we are principally focused on getting as close as possible to achieving our currently defined goals and objectives (and our operating numbers for the quarter or the year), it's just not very likely that we're going to look beyond those targets and over the horizon in order to see the less obvious and more extraordinary areas of possible change.

The truth is that we just don't have to do things in the same calculated and mechanical ways that we always have in the past and we especially don't have to construct the kinds of capital-intensive, costly and time-consuming foundations (including, but not limited to, every kind of bricks and mortar solution that is out there today) which were required and essential supports in the past, but which today simply constrain us and slow us down. This isn't simply that old familiar conversation to the effect that "we didn't need better buggy whips or faster horses, we needed cars"; it's an even broader commentary than that. We don't need the horses, we don't need the stables, and, frankly, any day now, we may not need the drivers themselves.

What we need is new inspiration and new approaches that are disruptive and discontinuous – not linear extensions – but true experiments with admittedly unknown outcomes and results, but which also represent the prospect of exponential potential gains. And the very good news today is that these types of new solutions can be implemented in less costly ways than ever before so that the real risks and downsides of continued experimentation can be constrained and largely mitigated.

It's also encouraging to see that these innovative approaches aren't limited to new businesses, but are being incorporated in the strategies of plenty of large and old line companies as well. Admittedly, in some cases, they are acting belatedly and defensively rather than leading the charge, but at least they are moving in the right direction. But whatever the age and size of your business, you need to be thinking about the steps you should be taking to distance and differentiate your products and services from both the competition you can see today and the much more threatening and extensive competition still to come. And, even more importantly, you need to ask yourself what – if anything – is the sustainable competitive advantage that you are hoping to create for your business so that it can compete in the future on anything other than price which is always a race to the bottom for any business.

No one can tell you the specific steps you will need to take to make these jumps, but here are two interesting and instructive cases which are worth continuing to watch in order to see how they might be applicable to your own situation. One is a done deal and one is an open question.

(1) <u>The Book Biz is About Anything But Books</u>

Please don't call anyone in the book biz a "publisher" these days just because – if you twist their arms – they might sell you a book. The "P" word is definitely out and the new industry buzzwords are all about adaptive learning and learning management systems, etc. Why is this seemingly semantic change so interesting? Because – for all intents and purposes – it reflects the decisions made by all of the biggest book publishers in the land to just throw in the towel and pretty much leapfrog right over the digital book business without even trying to explore those kinds of content offerings. It would appear that they're leaving the field wide open for Amazon and Apple, but maybe they know something that isn't obvious to the rest of us. There may not be any there there any longer.

If you ask them why they didn't aggressively pursue the protected digital distribution of their content, it turns out that their decisions weren't really based on the usual considerations which continue to plague the music and film industries – theft by pirates, cheap low-quality duplication, peer-to-peer sharing, etc. It turns out that they concluded that the intrinsic value of the content itself which they had to offer was being slowly ground down to nothing by: (a) the actions of the content creators themselves (rather than the actions of others as was the case in music and movies); (b) highly-efficient used book marketers; (c) the advent of MOOCs; and (d) free webcasting of lectures and classes by universities and professors all over the world - so they just decided to jump right over the challenging and unprofitable distribution game and move to building proprietary and protectable learning systems which they could market and sell to their same customers and which would assist in teaching whatever the content might be and, more importantly, measuring the results of those efforts.

(2) <u>A New Lease on Life for Libraries?</u>

Libraries aren't much better off than books these days and cities and schools of every size and shape are trying to figure out what the library of the future will look like and – very frankly – what real functions it will provide which justify its continued existence and provide some kind of differentiation from so many other public and private spaces. There are about 120,000 libraries in the U.S. these days and the vast majority (pretty close to 100,000) are in schools and universities. And you can be sure that in almost every instance, there are other users, groups, departments and facility management professionals who are coveting those large (and largely empty) spaces in their institutions for a million other uses. The one thing that we know for sure is that relying on "tradition" in order to support the old ways of doing things won't do the trick much longer. Tradition these days is just a delusion of permanence and - most often – it's just an easy excuse for those who don't want to change.

So the challenge that I would leave you with is to think creatively and disruptively about what will we do with our libraries now that books are increasingly a thing of the past? Should they simply be community spaces? Safe harbors for kids after school? Coaching and supplementary education places? Or just rows and rows of recycled desktops for accessing digital everything. Right now, this is a very open question. You should regard it - not as a closed book - but as a very large volume full of empty pages.

BUILD A BRIDGE, NOT ANOTHER BAND-AID

Paul Simon and Art Garfunkel had it right and they actually didn't even know it. I think that today they'd still probably be embarrassed if someone called them "computer geeks" or said that they had perfectly articulated the newest and smartest solution we've seen in some time for the legacy and enterprise-wide computer system problems that continue to plague many of the country's largest businesses. But the fact is that they said it all in a song.

The correct solutions today (and the enormous set of opportunities they create for smart young businesses) for a great deal of the legacy leftovers, remnant and orphaned protocols, and general "spaghetti code" confusion that continues to impede important process improvements, speed and efficiency enhancements, and any amount of material innovation in these big businesses are actually pretty simple. Some of these things are sitting there in plain sight, but they're overlooked by the guys who've been staring at the same stale whiteboards for years and retreading the same tired paths. Rehashing the same old stew isn't going to help anyone get ahead.

The simple answer - as the boys used to sing in the 70's – is all about building a "bridge over troubled water". It's not about trying to implement the latest desperate attempt (in a long, sad series of stop-gap measures and bulked-up bandages) which simply adds complexity to the current code base and postpones the necessary progress to the ultimate solution. You can't save your way to these kinds of radical solutions and you can't do it on the cheap either. But you won't get anywhere at all if you don't have a new and clear vision of where you're headed.

Here's the hard truth: the guys that got them there and built the problems that these companies are living with today aren't gonna get them to the next level of solutions. They're committed to their code with their embedded approaches and they're stuck trying to drag those ancient albatrosses forward into the future. It's a heavy load; it's the wrong strategy; and it's doomed to be more of the same under the best of circumstances. There's only one way you're headed if you're looking through the rear view mirror and that's backwards.

Frankly, to solve these kinds of problems, these companies need to get help and a fresh set of uninvested eyes from the outside and they need a strategy that builds a new, streamlined and simply sufficient solution right over the top of the problems (a "bridge") rather than another massive rewriting project that takes forever, costs a fortune, moves the same deck chairs around, and basically repaints the flagpole. Even the best Band-Aid is no bargain in the long run.

And what is very interesting is that these aren't cases where the new kids on the block are going to be suggesting new things to be doing or even new ways to do them – they're creating bypasses, express lanes and other new streamlined and fast channels to get the work done. They know the inputs; they know the desired outputs and results; and they're free to determine the least costly and most efficient ways to connect them. It's as easy as that once you get over the old news.

It all comes down to a simple realization, but it's one that's very difficult for the folks whose history is closely tied to what's been built in the past to admit. They need to acknowledge that their hard work and voluminous body of code can be readily and easily replicated and, in fact, efficiently superseded by simpler and more straightforward solutions. Today it's not about the size of the effort and the lines of code created; it's about speed and throughput and – as often as not – the simpler and more elegant the code, the faster the results generated and the happier the end users.

The trick for the old guys is not to take this stuff personally. No one said that life was fair or that anything lasted forever. And the trick for good managers is to acknowledge that the rules of the game have changed and – while it's not exactly fair – it's something that needs to be recognized and lived with.

The best approach (and it's still not an easy one) is to recognize and appreciate that the guys who built the ships that got us to this point were the explorers and the trailblazers and the real inventors in many cases, but their path was long and hard and costly and full of false starts, wrong paths, broken code, etc. along with plenty of do-overs. But they still got there and that's a true accomplishment and something to be respected.

Unfortunately now for them, whether it's fair or not, the new guys with the new eyes get the easy job – they already know where the goal line is and they know what works and what the users need and now they have a much easier job – they simply need to build a bridge that spans the old code and connects the past with the future as quickly and inexpensively as possible. And that's all about execution rather than exploration and that's what it's going to take to finally break out of the restrictions and legacies of the past in order to build the paths to the future.

The way forward isn't through the morass; it's over the top.

NO ONE WINS THE RACE
TO THE BOTTOM

Today, because the barriers to entry into almost any business are so low and the costs are so modest, competitors can be in your business and in your face in an instant. And because much of the Web is still very much like the Wild West, prospects and customers have very little accurate information to go on in making their initial choices and evaluations of various products or services.

Website and service validation businesses represent an entirely new and interesting digital marketplace and Stella Service is one of the early leaders in the space trying to become the "Good Housekeeping" seal of approval for e-commerce and other sites. It's a fertile opportunity and you can bet that he'll have plenty of competition in no time at all.

But, because the need is a real one, everyone will eventually be much better served and become much smarter decision-makers by virtue of the immediate access they will have to timely and accurate comparative information concerning everything they are thinking about buying, selling, using, visiting or consuming. We're about to enter the Mocial world.

Mocial is just a mash-up of mobile and social, but what it stands for is a much more complex and important set of ideas and requirements. Mocial means providing: (1) what we need; (2) when we need it; (3) wherever we are; and (4) without asking. Places and spaces will become intelligent and active and they will tell us relevant and particularized "stories" based on who we are, where we are and what we are doing as well as our prior contextual-sensitive activities and histories. Nudge commerce and next-generation suggestive selling systems will make a lot of the basic purchase decisions for us – especially in-store or online. Google Now is an early second-generation entrant into these kinds of services

However, for the moment, as a result of inadequate and poorly distributed marketplace information, false claims and promises, bait and switch offers, and cheap prices are far too prevalent on the Web and unfortunately they're disproportionately effective for the moment. And even though price and value are two radically different things, it's often very difficult for your company to make your case in the few moments or seconds during which you typically have the buyer's attention.

Worse yet, in today's Costco-fied economy, besides price, uber-size seems to matter most to too many consumers. Measuring bigger is easy. Measuring better is much harder because it requires judgment and values. But it's not all that clear that most consumers care about long-term value especially given the highly-disposable nature and prompt obsolescence of so many of today's products and services.

As a result, you can find yourself trying to keep up with and compete against new entrants and other competitors who really have no skin in the game. Having nothing, they have nothing to lose – all they can do is mess up the market for you. And like finding a turd in the punch bowl, once the prices start to spiral down, things only get uglier and less appetizing. There's really no way back.

This is also why - for a real player - it's no fun at all to play poker for pennies. Playing for peanuts (or with people with nothing to lose) takes away the pain and pressure of making difficult choices and sacrifices. But even that's only half the story. The other reason that it's a waste of time to play for pretend stakes is that there is no real impact outside of the game if you lose. Ultimately nothing is more important to good decision-making than the ability to identify, appreciate and evaluate the costs and consequences of our actions. Not, of course, just at the poker table, but in all our business relationships and in our lives in general as well.

And please don't buy into this noise about there being room for everyone in the market and that more players just expand the overall market size. Your job is to kill the competition – if they're about to drown; throw them a nice large anvil to speed the process along. They want your family to starve and your kids to be homeless.

And even if these mopes were worthy competitors instead of low-ball artists, trying to compete on price or sheer quantity - especially for a start-up - is a very tough and risky choice and almost always a bad idea. This is why you don't wrestle with pigs – you'll both get dirty, but only the pig will enjoy it.

Not only are there no winners in the race to the lowest price, it actually turns out that, for many of us today, even "free" isn't cheap enough. This is because in many cases the costs of usage and adoption have a lot more to do with the calculated allocation of scarce personal time and precious resources rather than with just dollars and cents. In addition, there are always other and better dimensions to compete on if you're really doing your job.

So, as tough as it can sometimes be, the best plan is to ignore the guys in the cheap seats and concentrate on making sure that you're delivering a product or service that's worth the prices you're asking your customers to pay. In the end, that's all that really matters and that's what will win in the long run.

SAAS CAN BE A PAIN IN THE ASS

The promise of the cloud can be very seductive and the adoption in every industry of cloud-based solutions provided - by and large - by new, young companies offering all manner of software as a service (SaaS) solutions continues to accelerate. The prospects of reduced capital expenditures and smaller IT staffs as well as ubiquitous access and perpetual uptime are very compelling for any business.

And while I realize that there are a few big, long-established players (like Salesforce.com) in the SaaS space; if you look carefully, most of the major and more substantial players have concentrated on infrastructure plays while most of the new, interesting, and potentially highly disruptive software solutions are being offered by young players who have elected to ride on that newly available infrastructure which is inexpensive to access (though not to build) and to assemble their products and service offerings on top of these industrial-strength platforms which are being provided by Amazon, Microsoft and others.

But those new young entrants present three serious and essentially structural risks to businesses looking to move to the cloud which every CEO needs to appreciate and evaluate before making such a move. The truth is that not every "cloud" has a silver lining and – as the head of a growing company – before you bet your entire business and begin to migrate mission-critical services and offerings to the cloud - you need to be sure (a) that you really understand who you're signing up with; (b) that you appreciate what you're signing up for and what you're not getting; and (c) that you have an accurate picture of the risks that you are taking and how they compare to the

<u>potential</u> benefits of a move. The devil is always in the details and, in many cases, the devil you know and have worked with for years (with all the warts and all the complaints) may still be a better bet for your business than a crapshoot on a company that's still getting its shit together.

Only after you get solid and complete answers to a few, very critical and important questions should you think about moving forward. These aren't easy things to determine or simple inquiries to make, but you won't get a second chance if you move prematurely or if you pick the wrong vendor/ partner. You could end up entirely out of business. So take the time and commit the resources to do the necessary due diligence and to look hard before you leap. They're called "clouds" for a reason – they're not remotely transparent – they're totally opaque.

Here are some brief thoughts on the three most critical concerns and one final suggestion:

Who Are These Guys and Are Their Interests Aligned with Mine?

When you're first starting out and trying to build a new business, there's a tremendous emphasis and tons of pressure on management to keep increasing revenues. Make the sale and move on to the next. But, for the customers, the rubber really meets the road when it's implementation time and that's when the SaaS sales guys tend to be long gone. And, because installations, training, configurations and the entire process of customization for individual users don't drive "new" revenues, the senior management and top sales guys at too many of these SaaS start-ups have little or no interest in these "down and dirty", but crucial parts of the migration process. I think that this is totally because they are focused solely on the top line and compensated accordingly.

But, even if you want to give them the benefit of the doubt, and you say that – because they've never done it before – they don't understand that software development is basically a business of brief moments of creation embedded in a lifetime of maintenance; it still doesn't make life any better or smoother for their customers. Essentially the basic SaaS *modus operandi* is to sell the stuff in and then leave the rest of the work to third party consultants and integrators or to the customer. Bottom line – they're into sales, not service or support, and you can easily end up – under the best of circumstances - with a partial solution and a load of headaches.

What Am I Getting and What Do I Only "Think" I'm Getting?

Not only is the SaaS solution sometimes half-delivered; it's also often half a loaf when you look under the hood. In some ways, it's a competitive advantage to be young enough not to know any better and not to know what you can't do. Entrepreneurs regularly bite off too much and promise far more than they can deliver. Business as usual – buyer beware – no harm, no foul. But other times, especially with first-generation software programs, the initial set of buyers are involuntarily turned into the last beta testers and – believe me – that doesn't make for happy campers. In this context, I like to say that SaaS software changes and upgrades aren't released; they escape from the engineers. Newbies seize on the "lean" methodology jargon as an excuse to launch all kinds of under-cooked and half-assed products, but we're all pretty tired of hearing that flaws are actually features, and not bugs. And, in addition, it turns out that, by "lean", they don't even mean simply-designed initial MVPs; they mean that they plan to learn what works and what doesn't by leaning on the users and letting them live through all the hiccups and mistakes.

Young entrepreneurs rarely understand the difference between a software program and a software product. Developing a robust and stable software product (with programs incorporated into it) which will hopefully be used by hundreds or thousands of customers in a wide variety of ways and contexts takes at least TEN times longer and far more effort than developing a basic software program or solution for a private user. This where all that nasty, time-consuming, and highly-detailed work called implementation, configuration and customization comes in which – by the way – rarely scales.

Are the Savings, Flexibility and New Functionality Worth the Risks to My Business?

Drivers of electric cars suffer from "range" anxiety. They worry about whether their current charge will last long enough to get home or to the next charging station. Thoughtful and attentive SaaS users should suffer constantly from "change" anxiety for two reasons. First, another portion of the half-a-loaf problem is that, as a SaaS customer (whether you realize it or not), you only get effective control over your part of the total package. This makes for the serious likelihood of some very nasty surprises whenever the main operating system in the cloud is changed, updated or otherwise revised – with or without ample notice to you and rarely with testing sufficient to confirm that the new versions will work with your install. Think of the overall installation as having two parts (theirs and yours) and ANY time that the two parts get out of sync, you're basically screwed.

Ultimately, I feel that the real problem is a structural one – the vendors are worried about enhancing and improving their main set of offerings and solutions and you're praying (because you've spent a small fortune configuring and customizing your end of their system so that it works with and for your business) that whatever changes they make won't damage or disrupt your operations. I hope that you don't think for a minute that there are ANY SaaS vendors out there who test their new updates and revisions against every customer's installation and usage BEFORE they release the new versions. That would be far too difficult and time-consuming as well as impossibly costly to staff and support.

And it gets worse. No small start-up can realistically afford (whether they admit it to you or not) to build and be running a completely separate development environment alongside their production systems. That's just not the way the world or the money works in the start-up universe. And, as a result, they release their changes into the production environment and – as noted above – they do their testing on you and your business in real time. This is the fundamental risk of a cloud-based solution. One size and one version or system will never work for any serious number of customers and frankly the attitude in the SaaS world isn't to make the system work for the customers. Once these businesses have any real traction and installed bases, their attitude is that you need to decide whether their system will work for you and – if it doesn't – they respectfully suggest that you change your business processes until it does.

One Last Thing to Think About

And remember one final thing – in addition to determining whether the vendor's sales people are telling you the truth and whether the references they provide are legitimate and satisfied users (or just fellow victims looking for company) - you have to weigh and consider the agendas and the motivations of the people <u>inside your company</u> as well. In every case I have seen (or suffered through myself), there are well-intentioned and sincere people on both sides of the decision with decent reasons to support their arguments and then there is usually another collection of people who are scared to make any decision that they might be blamed for; afraid to rock the boat or change things; committed to prior solutions that they endorsed or recommended; protecting their own job, people, turf or fiefdoms; and/or just too lazy to want to do the work that it takes to do one of these migrations well. They are rarely incented to give you the straight scoop.

Information (along with hard questions and sharp edges) has a way of getting smoothed out and softened as it wends its way upward in your organization on its way to your desk. That's just another fact of life – regardless of how big or little your headcount is. Just be sure you have all the facts before you make your move.

SOMETIMES GOOD ENOUGH IS GOOD ENOUGH

I spent some time recently with a very talented and thoughtful team of young entrepreneurs from Pathful (www.pathful.com) who were developing some new analytical tools to help non-technical website owners determine which parts of their websites were effective for them (driving engagement, conversion and ultimately sales) and which other parts either weren't as successful or, worse yet, were actually damaging to their business because they aggravated, frustrated or confused visitors and ultimately turned them off.

This is a bigger problem and a much bigger deal today for business owners than you might imagine (and, most likely, it's a problem for you as well) because – while everyone tells us (regardless of our size or type of business) that we need a website – no one (including the companies who build and host the websites) ever tells us (the site owners) with any precision or detail whether the website is really "working" for us and/or whether it's worth the time and investment which we've made (and continue to make) in it. Try it yourself. If you call up your website developer, provider or host today and ask how your site is doing, at best, you'll get some "up-time" data and maybe some traffic information, but nothing that really deals with the real metrics and ROI of the website.

As I learned more about this new business, one very appealing aspect of their SAAS-based service was how highly automated the back-end processing and reporting systems were going to be and how – as a result

– they could cost-effectively offer some basic versions of their products, services and reports at prices which would be reasonably affordable and which would appeal to early-stage businesses (as well as many Mom & Pop businesses) all of which they clearly understood wouldn't and couldn't afford or justify the costs of licensing and implementing some of the higher-end and much more expensive analytics packages which have been in the market for a while. Another of the best aspects of their new offerings was how quick and "easy" they said it would for a business to deploy their software and start getting valuable feedback. They simply had to "add a couple of lines of *Java* script" to their site and they were ready to roll. Just like implementing some of *Google's* basic tools.

And that's where I started to get worried that they were about to become victims of their own narrow environment and technical expertise. Because when you're sitting in a start-up incubator or a shared tech workspace killing it with your team and you're all surrounded by dozens (or even hundreds) of other smart, young techies who eat *Java* script for breakfast, it's a lot like living in an echo chamber lined with mirrors.

Everyone hears what they want and perhaps even what they need to hear in order to keep going, but - by and large - they simply have very little idea of how life actually works outside their bubble in the real (very pedestrian and non-technical) world. Especially if one of your prime market target sectors are young and small businesses. Telling a small business owner that all he needs to do is to "add a little code" to his website is a lot like handing him a pen knife and telling him that it's cheaper and easier to just do his own root canal. And he doesn't even need to make an appointment.

And there's a second, equally problematic, aspect of this type of situation which I call the "curse of creeping functionality". It's driven by talent and enthusiasm and the best of intentions, but it can really hurt a start-up by resulting in product offerings that are too complex and ambitious and way too over-engineered and technical for the larger market. They may suit and please the earliest adopters, but they're gonna freak out the crowd. The fact is that the "boys in the back room" just want to keep on building great code and adding more and more to the company's products, but here's the nasty news: new products and services have to satisfy the immediate needs of prospective customers and current users and not the egos or desires of the company's managers and engineers.

For so many companies today that are tech-based, this is a really difficult growth phase to navigate and it can easily lead to hurt feelings, abrupt departures of key employees and plenty of other problems including a lot of passive-aggressive behavior and foot-dragging from the geeks. But if you're the CEO and you're building the right kind of business, then you've also got to be the customers' and users' advocate; rein in the troops; and make sure that your products meet the market's needs and not the other way around.

Existing users are incrementalists – they are generally at least willing to try system enhancements and updates as long as these are not disruptive of their ongoing activities. New prospects, on the other hand, are always looking for an easy on-ramp and a simple way to start. They don't want to read a book, take a training course, or spend a week getting up to speed – they just want to get started. For the vast majority of customers, too many bells and whistles (products that "can do whatever you want") are not attractive enticements or incentives; they're perceived headaches and anticipated heartburn in the making. Prospects and new customers don't want tools that can do "anything" – that's not a meaningful or useful concept for them – in fact, it's most often off-putting and too vague to help convince them of anything. Basically, they want solutions to serious, finite and obvious needs that they have to solve pressing problems which are important to them. Now I will admit that they may not even know that they have some of these problems until they're "sold" on the need for a solution, but I can also promise you that they want a solution in a box and not a set of D.I.Y. instructions telling them how to build the scaffolding and infrastructure that they'll need to solve their problems.

Now, don't get me wrong. For many companies with the right staff and support, adding a powerful, effective and inexpensive tool like this to their website would be a no-brainer and a very smart thing to do. I understand that not everything can be natural, easy, user-friendly and taste like chocolate. But for the millions of little guys all over the country who really need and could benefit from this kind of objective, third-party review of the value and effectiveness of their sites, identifying the problem for them, but then offering them only a partial solution which they can't take advantage of or implement themselves is a waste of everyone's time and effort.

And yet, if you step back and really look at what the customer's problem is that you are trying to solve (what's the "job" that needs to get done) rather than getting locked into a perspective of focusing on all the great things your new service and software can do and create, it's actually pretty easy to figure out a better answer and a much better offering. In this particular case, the problem is very clear: if the customer is paralyzed or afraid or incapable of adding the couple of lines of simple code to his website, you've got to figure out how to add it remotely (or through a channel partner like BrightTag www.brighttag.com) for him. Once it's there, everything else is easy. I'm thinking something along the lines of a next-generation, no-brainer *InstallShield* kind of download that the customer just emails to the host of his site although an interesting question is whether those gatekeepers are gonna be happy to help or pains in the ass to get around.

Basically, you've got to solve the WHOLE problem for these little guys and, once you figure out how to do that, you discover that there's a huge, readily scalable market sitting right in front of you. And as long as you entirely solve at least part of the problem, it's not critical at the outset that your solution does everything, addresses all the issues, provides every form of report, etc. That can all come later – but only if you can get a foot or two in the door and get started. This is really what disruptive innovation is all about – start small, listen aggressively, iterate and then scale.

And the best part of this approach is that, once you can eliminate the major barrier to acceptance (the *Java* script addition to the website in this case) and get yourself onboard, you discover that the bar for substantial success is embarrassingly low. Sometimes simple is more than sufficient for a large segment of the market. Good enough in this case can be more than good enough. You can make this low-end, high-volume, automated version of your product or service easier, simpler, and less robust, etc. because these companies aren't power users or sophisticated buyers; they're customers who would be grateful for any help in this area. And the more hand-holding, explaining, and straightforward analysis that you can do for them, even at the most basic level, the more appreciative and satisfied they will be.

DON'T BUILD YOUR BIZ
ON A PINNACLE

It used to be a sign of disrespect and condemnation to say that someone had their head in the clouds. They were foolish dreamers or cock-eyed optimists - certainly not the kind of down-to-earth folks firmly grounded in reality that anyone with any brains would want to bet on and/or invest in. Thoreau wrote about people building castles in the air (which he said was where they should be), but then he cautioned that the next steps needed to be putting solid foundations under them.

Right now, you can't go anywhere without hearing or seeing another pitch for SaaS and enduring multiple arguments for putting your products and services in the cloud. I wrote about SaaS not too long ago myself although my view – then as now – was a pretty contrary one. (See: Why SaaS is More Dangerous than It Looks. http://www.inc.com/howard-tullman/why-saas-is-more-dangerous-than-it-looks.html). As it happens, being in the cloud today is supposed to be way cool. Everyone will tell you that it's definitely the place for your business to be. But I'd say "maybe". Because I think it depends entirely on what kind of business you're planning to build and whether you've built the right foundation for moving forward.

This is because sometimes - especially in the world of technology - you learn that the more things seem to change, the more they stay the same and you eventually realize that they're no different than they've always been. I don't want to rain on anyone's parade, but the cloud's no more a panacea and the answer to all things than any of the other wondrous tools and technologies that came before it. The cloud can kick-start you or kill you if you're not careful. And sadly, if your head's stuck up there in the haze and you think the cloud's gonna solve everything for you and your business, you're likely to be just as mistaken and wrong-headed today as you would have been years ago which was – by the way - long before we all discovered the supposedly silver linings inside all those newly-accessible and suddenly transparent clouds.

If your business plan and model are appropriate, the cloud could be a big help, but if your model makes no sense, nothing including the cloud will make much of a difference. Because when you really look closely, you discover that the cloud's not magic or another Oz – it's just a virtual place in cyberspace - an environment to operate in - and for your startup to be successful anywhere - in the ether or down on Earth - you've still got to build a business that's well-grounded and smart. There's no question that the cloud's cheap and easy in many ways, but there are plenty of things that you just shouldn't ever do for your business and trying to do them cheaply is much worse than not doing them at all. So it pays to do your homework before you head into the ozone. And, in particular, that's why, when you're thinking about the cloud and your business model, it's so important to pay attention to exactly what you're trying to build.

Pinnacles are a Problem

Pinnacles are generally very tall and relatively thin. They're a very precarious foundation for a business because they don't provide a broad base of user engagement or commitment or support and they really limit your ability to connect to your customers and, more importantly, to react to and/or cushion the impact of adverse developments. The cloud encourages us to chase the world and boil the ocean from Day One because those opportunities are theoretically there for the taking. But, if you fall for the long thin line (essentially the polar opposite of the long tail), you find that you're stretched way out (a mile high and an inch wide) and that a relatively modest upset, piece of bad news, or other disturbance can really knock your whole enterprise off course because your real connection to so many of your remote and very distant customers is so tenuous. To build a smart business, you never want to be spread too widely or have too thin a connection to your users and this is how I see a number of businesses today.

You want to be focused, but not single-threaded – you want to be straight, but not narrow – and you always want to have a couple of ways out of the tight spots. And it's pretty easy to drink your own Kool-Aid if you're not careful. For example, if you're disrupting and revolutionizing an industry where the standards of response time and performance were historically measured in days or weeks, you don't have to introduce your new solution and your initial metrics in terms of minutes or hours of turn-around time. Give yourself a break and some breathing room. It's always easier to improve than to walk the customers back from some insane, unscalable and hyper-costly benchmark that you simply made up.

This is an area where too much information – being too data-driven – can actually limit your opportunities and your upside while increasing your vulnerability because you can fall in love with the measurements and lose sight of the critical relationships and your real business objectives. Take measuring turn-around or response times (as noted above) or tracking geographic penetration as examples.

Measurement is a relativist thing and when we are constantly measuring our results against purely pre-defined goals and objectives, it's too easy to develop a case of tunnel vision. As the data tell us that we are drawing ever nearer to the goal ("our uptime is great and our response time is terrific") and we convince ourselves that we're getting better and better ("we have customers in 50 countries"), we lose sight of the fact that (a) these may be easy things to measure, but they aren't necessarily the important things to focus on or optimize for the long run; (b) too much of a good thing probably isn't a good thing if it's too soon to manage it; and (c) there may be much larger and broader opportunities over the horizon and outside of our immediate zones of interest and – while we're feeling so good about our near-term progress – someone else is out there getting ready to steal the main prize out from under us.

Because the cloud can so readily and inexpensively connect us to many or just a few users everywhere and because it enables degrees of unimaginable and constant connectivity, it is very seductive and it's very easy to run down these rabbit holes and lose your way. You can quickly end up over-extended, under-manned and unable to meet the commitments you've made to your users and customers. It's pretty lonely and uncomfortable sitting on top of that pinnacle wondering what went wrong. But at least it's not crowded.

NOTHING'S MORE POWERFUL
THAN A PLATFORM

People casually talk about "the cloud" as a platform, but it's not. It's just an alternative method of data conveyance. Most simply stated, it's a part of the pipe that gets you to and from whatever platform (think resource repository) you're looking for where you can access, connect to, interact with, and/or extract whatever you need. The cloud has solved the classic distribution dilemma which has dogged millions of young businesses since the beginning of time. How do I get my product or service offering out there to the masses? Solving that riddle is far more possible today through multiple channels – especially the app stores – than ever before.

In the old days, the name of the game used to be all about location. But in today's hyper-mobile world of constant connectivity, location is essentially immaterial (work itself is also no longer place-based) and effective distribution is all that matters. The cloud (basically for free to the end user) makes access ubiquitous and response time close to instantaneous. This is compelling and tremendously helpful (as well as cost-effective), but the real value and the ultimate power still resides with the parties who control the contents and the underlying delivery platform itself – not in the pipes. We see tiny, but very clear examples of the relative power of the players every time some cable company tries to extort additional carriage fees from content providers. All these games eventually end up in the same way – the guys with the goods get the gold – and the pipe guys are sent packing and back to the woodshed.

But when I talk about platforms, I'm not talking about the basic technology platforms (iOS6, Jelly Bean or Windows 8) that run our devices; I'm talking about the data, content and transaction platforms (or you might think of them as bi-lateral networks) which are sitting on top of these enabling technologies and which connect us with the data we desire, cool content of every kind, necessary products and services or simply other people.

And by the way, if you're wondering why there are only 3 mobile platforms (actually 2 ½ to be honest); that will tell you something important in itself about the power of platforms. Platforms are central to the "winner-take-all" realities of the world of technology and they help to create the inevitable concentration in these markets where one or two winners outdistance the field and then enjoy disproportionate and substantial profits for as long a time as their dominance persists. And these windfall and excess profits – if aggressively deployed – can further accelerate the ability of the leaders to pull away from the pack in many different ways. Excess cash can be applied to securing priority positions and placements in critical channels, crowding the channels themselves and closing out available ad inventory or other exposure available for competitors, predatory pricing, etc.

The fact is that, in markets fundamentally driven and dominated by (a) two or three central platforms, (b) mission-critical technologies, (c) ubiquitous operating systems; (d) enabling networks; or (e) products with very little, possibly zero, marginal production and distribution costs; over some reasonably short period of time, there will consistently emerge a clear and obvious winner, a strong number two and then a bunch of midgets and also-rans. There's just not enough volume or oxygen in these intensely competitive markets to support a half dozen winners. All of the structural considerations inherent in the ways we (as customers and consumers) elect to narrow and concentrate our choices rather than broadening the scope of our inquiries and our horizons also help to reinforce and precisely dictate the result we see over and over again in these case. Whether it's time constraints, an interest in efficiency, pure ignorance, sheer laziness or just basic human nature, we all tend to pick (and stick with) our familiar favorites.

There are a number of other contributing factors to this recurring outcome which are less personal – demonstrated economies of scale, market-dictated centralization and standardization requirements, and, of course, the power of Metcalfe's Law which first described and defined the exponential growth characteristics of networks and how that growth rapidly increased the network's power, resilience and value. The more power and connections a business had to and with its users, the more powerful and profitable it would become.

Metcalfe's law with certain subsequent refinements and embellishments stated that the value of any network (originally consisting of connected and bilaterally communicating inanimate devices, but these days counting nodes of any kind including people and/or users) was proportional to the square of the number of connections. If anything, in today's world of constant connectivity where every one of us is tethered to one or more devices at all times, the predictive power and nearly universal application of Metcalfe is even more relevant.

So your mission is pretty clear. If you want to find the prime position for your business to capture value from whatever back-and-forth activity is going on in your industry; you're going to want to identify the convergence points within the market – through which virtually all of the traffic and commerce needs to pass – and that's where your business needs to be. If you can locate the hub (not the spokes) and get yourself on the gatekeeper gravy train; you will learn very quickly just how powerful a position this can be. Being paid even a little something every time anything moves over a network adds up to a whole lot of everything in pretty short order.

And here's the deal: you don't have to be some Colossus astride the harbor to pull this off. Smart little guys can often construct effective horizontal platforms more quickly and economically than the big vertical (and siloed) players who dominate many (mainly oligopolistic) markets. You just need to understand the basic building blocks and the dynamics of what makes a particular platform prevail. And you need to plan to be a platform from Day One. Believe me, it's not something you stumble into.

So what do you need to know and be thinking about in terms of creating a persistent and winning platform as you try to build and properly position your own business?

(1) Do Something for the Market that the Major Players Can't Do Collectively or for Themselves

There are any number of industries where the major players are prevented by law or regulations from collaborative or cooperative efforts (very often these laws specifically target pricing issues) which are almost automatically regarded by the authorities and regulators not as helpful, but as predatory, exclusionary and anti-competitive. This makes it very difficult to structure and organize some market solutions that might ultimately be very beneficial and cost-effective for the consumer and which – at least arguably - ought to be of equal interest and concern to the same regulators. At the same time, these situations create great opportunities and openings for little guys to come out of nowhere and create sustainable new solutions.

So, in the case of the book publishers and Apple (albeit at Amazon's urging), the government attorneys have sued, fined and/or settled with almost all of the players for "conspiring to fix book prices". But, in the streaming music space, (where the music moguls seem to have finally learned a few lessons from the Napster debacle), we have Spotify and Shazam and others providing new services to consumers. And guess what? By creating industry-wide platforms for music delivery, these aggressive little startup companies not only blew the big guys away, but – even better yet – invited them in as investors. At last count, Spotify investors included: Sony BMG at 5.8 percent, Universal Music at 4.8 percent, Warner Music at 3.8 percent and EMI at 1. 9 percent. Also Merlin holds a small stake. The story is pretty much the same with Shazam where Sony, Universal (Vivendi) and Warner (Access Industries) each invested the exact same amount of $3 million. Could the message they are sending be any clearer? A very convenient and "legal" way for the very same guys who couldn't do it themselves to do it together thru smart startups building next-gen platforms.

(2) Create Criteria or Objective Benchmarks that Become the De Facto Industry Standards

A second path to becoming an industry platform deals with a different issue that again is common in many industries and presents new opportunities in all of them. In markets dominated by a few majors, a common problem in organizing and improving the efficiency of the market and creating better visibility (and "apples-to-apples" price comparison capability) for consumer is the lack of common and consistent nomenclature and the fact that each of the players has adopted and is psychologically "stuck" with their own numbering, identifying and classifying systems for their products even though the products offered by multiple players are functionally and often physically identical.

There are a lot of reasons for this – companies that believe that their branding and reputation will permit them to charge the consumer more for a product that is basically a commodity come to mind as the type of player which will resist market standardization. But they are basically losers (or will shortly be) in the new world of transparency where even the laziest consumer willing to do the minimal amount of research can access almost perfect pricing data in a flash. Another reason for the resistance to change and improved market organization and efficiency is simply company pride of authorship and the "not invented here" syndrome. This is "how we do it" and we always will do it this way – flash – until the market tells them otherwise by moving quickly away from them. And a final complication is simple overkill. Many companies for reasons ranging from tradition to the requirements of antiquated legacy accounting and control systems have way too much information associated with every product in their inventory and accounting systems. This does nothing good for anyone and, in fact, creates additional impediments to the company's speed, competitive responses to changed market conditions, etc.

Not surprisingly, the solutions which are changing markets like these are again being created by startups who are unhampered by all the historical and traditional concerns (as well as the ego issues) that make it hard to innovate and improve the old ways of doing things in the big businesses that dominate these industries.

And, in addition to being free of the constraints of the past, these startups bring a fresh approach which can best be described by three critical words: "Good Enough Is". They aren't trying to write the Magna Carta for product classification or the Geneva Convention (worthless as that may be in its own right) for generating inventory lists; they are just interested in building a simple new solution that spans horizontally across the many market players and focuses only on the common and critical components and characteristics that matter to the market when specifications and purchase decisions are being made. Nothing needs to be perfect – nothing needs to be the "be-all and the end-all" – the solution that gets you started just needs to work and be good enough to get the job done. Things can and will always get better, but they won't ever happen if you don't get something started in the first place.

Need a simple example? Think about eBay way back when. No real product specifications. No serial numbers and other details. Not even photos in many cases at the beginning. But it became a powerful trading platform in very short order because it was a sufficient system to get the required job done. While customer expectations are definitely progressive over time; they're pretty primitive and modest at the outset of a new experience.

(3) Offer the End Users/Customers Independent and Consistent Evaluation Documentation

A third type of platform is one which creates a resource for buyers and sellers to access accurate, independent, and consistent documentation about the location, availability and costs of various products (often used or refurbished) which is not often available from the sellers or manufacturers of new equipment. In theory, the best type of platform for this particular need would be an active marketplace, but because it is often difficult and time-consuming to assemble a critical mass of buyers and sellers at the outset and sufficient transaction volume as well – the marketplace is a nice and desirable tool for generating the pricing and supply/demand data about various products – but it's not necessarily the only solution in the short term.

Better and more accurate information is always preferable, but in some cases, any information that helps the parties make smart and more informed choices is better than nothing. When I started CCC Information Services in 1980, the goal was exactly this – to provide in digital formats better, more accurate, and more timely information about used car prices for insurance adjusters and ultimately for consumers to use in settling insurance loss claims. 35 years later, the same basic platform that I built back then is still in use and CCC is still the industry leader in the insurance vehicle valuation space.

What's so great about working with innovative startups every day at 1871 is that I get to see new and exciting game-changing examples of businesses addressing some of the same issues I dealt with decades before, but applying them to new markets and opportunities. One case in point is MarkITx (an early 1871 company) which is building a platform to permit Fortune 1000 companies to efficiently value and then buy or sell the billions of dollars of used IT equipment that they have to update and dispose of every year.

Right now, in 90% of the cases, my impression is that the only important consideration for these companies is getting rid of the old stuff (someway, somehow) in order to quickly make room for the new stuff. The fact that they regard it as "junk" and that they have foolishly written the equipment down far too quickly on their books results in them leaving tens of millions of dollars on the floor of the shipping dock while some junk dealer drags the old stuff away.

A system like the one MarkITx is already putting in place for major firms with enormous dated equipment inventories that simply and accurately not only shows them the actual residual value of the pieces that they were about to pitch, but then also painlessly enables them to sell those items for cash on the barrel head has been a long time coming. But it's here now. And, just as you would expect, once you've got your shop set up on this kind of an automated system with a disposal schedule, etc. and you can just look forward to the "found money" rolling back into your coffers on a regular basis, you don't even think about doing something else or going elsewhere.

(4) Invest Your Resources in Infrastructure Individual Market Players Couldn't Justify or Afford to Create for Themselves

Another of the opportunity spaces for platforms are in markets not dominated by a few big guys, but consisting instead of a million little guys – none of whom are in a position to make the commitment or the capital investments (as well as absorbing the people costs) of funding the costs involved in launching, marketing and operating a central organizing platform for their industry or marketplace. As I said above, platforms don't happen accidentally and getting the word out about a centralized and ubiquitous utility platform is very tough and very expensive.

I'm somewhat surprised that even sophisticated business journalists often don't really get what's going on in these spaces. One writer whose opinions I generally respect commented on Uber and said he wasn't even sure that Uber was a technology company. He acknowledged that they used smartphones, but so, he said, did every other business these days including taxi companies. Frankly, he just didn't understand that it wasn't about the phone you used, it was all about the classic Ghostbusters question. Who ya gonna call? That's the name of the platform game. Sure everyone in the city could just call some random cab company on their phone from wherever they happened to be and hope for the best, but that's not a solution that anyone with any smarts thinks is a winner.

To solve this riddle, you've got to be top of mind with the consumer; have immediately responsive city-wide coverage; have a critical mass of participating drivers – 24/7; build a system to instantly connect them all thru a single distributed platform; and <u>then</u> have lots of cash and staying power and hope for the best. Anyone who thinks this isn't a technology business won't know a Tesla from a Model T.

So, at the end of the day, one thing is absolutely clear. It will be the companies driving and controlling the centralized and coordinated connections we need through the hubs, the networks, and the other emergent channels which will be the ones which can extract market-driven premiums from the communications, transactions and commerce moving through them. These gatekeepers (many of them startups who built the critical platforms) will keep a very fair share of the gold. Nothing primes a platform.

HOW RIDESCOUT GOT IT RIGHT

Way back when, in April of 2013, Scott Case and I participated in a rapid pitch program called Enrich Your Pitch at the INC. GROWCO conference in New Orleans. The competition featured all veteran-owned and operated businesses as the presenting companies. It was an impressive group and I was especially taken with an eager guy named Joseph Kopser who was pitching his relatively new business, Ridescout. At the time, I didn't realize quite how new it was.

Joe didn't win the grand prize, but he says that the press and the exposure from the event were worth their weight in gold from investors and helped him keep afloat and raise crucial funds at a very precarious time. He also told me - much more recently - that - at the time of his GROWCO pitch - he barely had a beta version of his idea and he was having an impossible time hanging on to users. In any event, we hit it off in the Big Easy and have been in regular touch ever since.

Now flash forward about a year or so, and Joe picks a luncheon at 1871 in Chicago as the place to launch Ridescout in the Midwest. The business literally exploded after that event into another 66 cities in a matter of weeks. It was a spectacular rollout and Joe has been running around the country ever since with 69 total active markets and several hundred ride providers. I thought I knew exactly what his game plan was – in fact – I wrote about the basic components of the strategy in two recent INC. columns about the power of platforms which are described below, but I still wanted to hear it from the horse's mouth.

Luckily for us, Joe still finds time to swing by his 1871 Chicago office on a regular basis and, most recently, in addition to promoting Ridescout, he's become a vocal and very active supporter of a new initiative that we have launched at 1871 called The Bunker which is an incubator and support program for veteran-owned businesses with a particular focus on technology. The Bunker is led by Todd Connor who is a Navy man and it launched formally a few weeks ago as part of the 1871 2.0 expansion program. We were honored to host the event which was attended by over 300 interested supporters, members, investors and vets as well as by U.S. Senator Dick Durbin, the senior senator from Illinois. And, of course, Joe was there at the Bunker launch as well because giving back and helping out is also a big part of who he is and what he wants to do with his life.

And then – just a couple of weeks later – came the big announcement that Daimler, one of the world's largest car manufacturer, had acquired Ridescout and entered the ride-sharing business. Quite another impressive step up for a startup that was scrambling to survive a little more than a year ago, but that's how it happens if you're in the right place with the right team and the right idea at the right time. And, of course, it never happens by accident.

So I sat down recently with Joe to ask him exactly what the secrets were to that drove the rapid national expansion and brought about all the good things that followed. And, in a word, he said that he basically built a "platform" which, of course, was music to my ears and exactly what I had assumed. And it's amazing how closely his description on the critical building blocks mirrored my recent INC. pieces.

What the Power of the Platform Means for Your Company covered parts 1 and 2 of the strategy: (a) do what the big guys can't do for themselves or won't do by working together; and (b) create de facto industry standards that organize otherwise unstructured data and markets.

Joe figured out early on that each of the alternative transportation providers was operating in a silo and the last thing that any of them cared about or was focused on was cooperating on sharing route and cost data - even if such a combination was clearly desired and highly valuable and beneficial for the end user. Basically, Ridescout built the bridge between these islands and created a comprehensive platform that served the consumer's needs.

Even more importantly, Joe understood that each vendor had their own language, terminology, interfaces, etc. and that the absolutely last thing any consumer needed were more individual apps on their phones which didn't talk to each other and which couldn't even be effectively compared with one another without investing an inordinate amount of time and energy.

The need for a one-stop shopping experience and an integrated solution was clear, but no one was really in a position to get the job done. Needless to say, the first mover would have a major shot at organizing the entire space, setting the industry standards, and becoming the market leader. Ridescout rode to the rescue.

The Primacy of the Platform dealt with the third major consideration: invest your energy and resources in building infrastructure that the individual players in a given market can't afford to do by themselves.

So the need was clear and there was a major opportunity, but Joe also needed to assemble the technical team that could get the job done quickly and in a fashion that was immediately scalable. He needed to build a platform and an overall solution that accomplished 4 things:

1. It was absolutely critical to figure out how to translate, aggregate and normalize the data which needed to be "grabbed" from sites, suppliers and vendors from all over the country into a consistent set of formats. Building the ingest tools and the translation programs were major time and dollar investments.

2. It was equally important to build a single interface for all sharing by vertical – in other words – all bike shares needed to ultimately look the same thru Ridescout regardless of the city you were in – and the same was true for all car shares, transit and rides for hire. No one else was stepping up to fund the development of a single standard and one which also needed to somehow account for the outliers in certain areas whose particular approaches needed to be melded into the overall system.

3. The system and the backend had to be scalable and robust enough on Day One to accommodate the flood of data (and hopefully users)

as well as demand from newly interested participating vendor and partners – once they woke up – on a national basis and the process needed to be as automated as possible.

4. The overall solution set needed to be extensible and always backwardly compatible because the only way to make sure that Ridesout maintained its leadership position was to constantly be raising the bar by adding features and functionality that responded to the input, suggestions, complaints and increasing demands and expectations of all the participants including the various governmental bodies in each geographic location. As it happened, the fact that Ridescout took a very conciliatory and collaborative approach to the city managers and regulatory bodies as they moved from market to market turned out to create a very substantial barrier for other potential new entrants.

Ultimately, time will tell, but Joe's off on an exciting and exploding ride and nothing beats a well thought-out and a well-built platform as long as you keep raising the bar.

YOU ARE WHAT YOU ARE
INTERESTED IN

When Facebook bought Karma (one of the leading gift sites) at the end of 2012, it was pretty clear that we were going to see a second iteration of Facebook Gifts - especially as the holiday shopping season started to heat up. Socially-informed commerce in various forms and shapes has been around for quite a while, but we're at another major inflection point now because of the impact of hyper-personalization and the far more precise and cost-effective targeting which is now available.

Keep in mind that it's a long-established principle that, if you give a consumer too many choices, they are far more likely to buy nothing than if you give them a limited and more relevant decision set. New young companies like Chicago-based Local Offer Network are jumping into this particular space as well with tools that deliver the "exactly right" offers to consumers visiting a site even the first time that the visitor appears. I call this "smart reach" and Facebook will be all over it – especially with Facebook Exchange.

Given the tools and resources that Facebook increasingly has at its disposal, they can now make the gift selection and giving process far more successful for the donor and also make the recipient far more likely to be happy with the gift. Remember that the excellence of a gift lies in its appropriateness, not simply in its value. And there are other important ancillary benefits as well. One of the reasons people get divorced is that they run out of gift ideas. Ergo – better gifts – less divorces.

So there's no question that this latest foray into "f-commerce" is going to be a big focus for the Facebook team along with a couple of other "interest graph-driven" initiatives like Facebook "Collections" which is their initial salvo in response to the explosive growth of Pinterest. If you want to get some idea of how interesting and accurate gift giving becomes when it's informed by detailed data about the interests and preferences and buying history of the friends and peers for whom you're trying to select a present, take a look at shopycat.com which is actually a product created by Wal-Mart Labs - but very cool nonetheless.

If you are more of a metrics person, here are some numbers to keep in mind – when a "friend" refers and/or recommends that someone they know take an action on the web – the impact (as compared to a simple ad solicitation) is major: recipients are 15% more likely to download something; 8% more likely to buy something; and – most importantly – when they do buy, the average order size is 22% larger. That's a lotta lift.

What's less obvious about the new gift-giving initiatives (the Lightbank/Groupon gang also invested in Boomerang in 2012 which is another gift site) is that, from Facebook's perspective, the dollars generated from gift purchases may be nowhere near as valuable in the long run to their enterprise as the purchase decision data which will be made available through these transactions as well as the implicit and explicit "connections" which each and every gift transaction will establish between their members. You can just imagine the opportunities for follow-on sales and service and the cross-marketing possibilities that each gift will create.

As I like to say, "personal data is the oil of the digital age" and Facebook increasingly owns the primary pump. And because birds of a feather flock together, other analytical tools will help correlate purchases with the buyer's presence in defined communities and other likely behavioral groups. Data, data and more data with virtually no acquisition cost and high degrees of precision and accuracy.

So the real "news" about Facebook Gifts is that we're continuing to see more and more indications of the next major seismic shift from the relatively simple social graph to the deeper interest graph. Because we (and Facebook in particular) have pretty much cracked the code on personal data and demographics (empowered in real-time by high-velocity computing), the next hurdle is pretty clear: "tell me what you're interested in and what you pay attention to and I will tell you who you are". And basically, if you're not where your targets and customers are and a relevant part of their world, you're nowhere. This is really where both Instagram, Aviary and Pinterest loom large.

As we see better and better tools to interpret and identify (and categorize) visual materials (photos and other images with videos to follow in the near future), we will see more and more emphasis on and influence of the players who are successfully aggregating these huge treasure troves of visual information. After all, a picture's worth about a million words these days if it's the right picture.

And speaking about the future and gifts reminds me that the future isn't a gift, it's an achievement that we work for and earn every day. Hard work is what makes our dreams come true.

But Facebook really is like a powerful steamroller and it rarely stops changing the rules of the game - and thereby - the world that we all live in today. The addition of Facebook Graph Search is really another major brick in the wall. But it's really a double-edged sword that will take some serious getting used to.

I've been worried for a while about the filter bubble and how narrow the search process was becoming as it increasingly morphed from a window on new worlds to a mirror reflecting back to us basically what we and our friends already know. Our peers are important, but how would you learn anything new if search was simply an endless loop?

I was also concerned about the death of serendipitous discovery which is the sheer joy we feel at a bookstore (remember those?) or a flea market (remember those?) when we come across something new and amazing and totally unexpected and it just makes our day. You didn't even know you were looking for something, but you loved it when you found it. And, of course, in search terms, you could never have constructed a query to find something you weren't seeking.

That's why I'm excited about Graph Search and why it will actually enable and enhance a lot of businesses (besides Facebook's) which could include yours once you understand some of the basics beneath the buzz.

First and foremost, GS is a return to the earliest days and, in fact, to the origin of Facebook. Think about it (even if you've only seen the movie) – it was about finding pictures of the hottest women on campus. And, clearly, it wasn't about women you knew (search); it was about women you wanted (desperately) to know (discovery).

GS takes the blinders and the filters off of the painstaking process of conscious search (does anyone really want to check out all of your friends' profiles one at a time?) and opens up a huge amount of additional social and personal and interest material that was always there, but which is now readily accessible. Broad content queries constrained by the limiters and filters of your friends is an elegant way to get right to the heart of the interest graph.

Two simple examples – how much better would a *Groupon* deal do if in 10 seconds I could ask Facebook which of my friends were already participating in the deal? Or have *Ticketmaster*'s concert seating charts (enabled by Facebook integration) show me which of my friends already have tickets to the show and where they are sitting?

So, as you start to think about how to position your business and your product and service offerings in new ways to make them discoverable and sharable thru the new power of Graph Search, keep in mind the following three aspects of GS:

(1) Aggregation

GS does the heavy lifting for you and assembles the data and results of your friends' likes, preferences and interests across whatever cuts and selections you care to make and permits you to interactively build on your questions and broaden or narrow them on the fly. Single friends with MBAs who are living in San Francisco and working in the entertainment business? You got it in a flash.

(2) Filters

Instead of limiting your queries or your results in the background in ways that were never really clear, filters now take on a new ability to help you frame your selections, criteria and choices in ways that avoid overwhelming and unwieldy results and permit you to dictate limits of scope, time, location, images, etc. Friends who loved *Inglourious Basterds* and are actually up for going to see *Django* with me? Try that on Google.

(3) Engagement

For now, and this may change, assets like photos are "valued" and ranked and displayed in engagement order which – in Facebook terms – means that the more likes and comments a particular photo has, the more likely it will be to be surfaced. The reason I think that this criteria is in flux is that it's highly likely that the volume of activity around a photo may be exactly why it's the least likely photo that the person shown in the photo wants circulated.

We're headed into the next big burst of Facebook-enabled commerce (f-commerce) and increasingly millions of customers are going to be living within this Facebook economy and nowhere else. If you doubt that, just check out how many times the Facebook team during the launch events repeated the idea that "you never have to leave Facebook" to do anything that you want to do.

Each of these components of the new GS engine will change many of the ground rules for how (and whether) new and small businesses will be able to make themselves heard and get their messages out to their prospective customers in the clutter and the crowd. It's not going to be easier, but it will definitely be more interesting.

Here's one last word of advice. One of the great internal mantras of Facebook regarding the creation of all social web content is: what will make them care? and what will make them share? As you bring your products and services to market, keep these two questions top of mind.

GOOGLE'S GROWING APP GAP

Two weeks ago was the 25th anniversary of the World Wide Web. Even for those of us who were there at the very beginning, it's hard to remember a time before the Internet. But the sad truth is that the Web, as we once knew it, is disappearing right before our eyes. Does anyone type "www" as part of an URL anymore? Does anyone type a URL anymore or really want to type anything? I think not.

We'd rather swipe a screen or press a button on our phone or, better yet, just tell our phone what it is that we need. In fact, whether we like to admit it or not, we'd actually much prefer for our devices to "know" what we need before we ask based on our preferences, interests, location, prior behaviors and profiles. Then, without having to ask, we'd just have the answers handy and readily available when, where and whenever we need them. I call this modality "MOCIAL" – the merger of mobile and social – which is driven and enabled by constant connectivity, high-velocity computing, and by the massive stores of data about all of us which are now accessible to virtually anyone at little or no cost. These new capabilities and tools set standards of speed and performance as well as expectations of immediacy and accuracy that even the very best websites can't hope to compete with. And the competitive bar just keeps rising. The truth is that we're all suckers for speed and simplicity – save me time and make me more productive and I'm yours.

Today's reality is that websites are pretty much yesterday's news and the vast majority (to the extent that they haven't already been practically abandoned by their owners) are destined very shortly to be orphaned or consigned to the virtual dustbin. They're slow on a good day and too often plagued by latency issues; they're fundamentally static rather than interactive; far too many <u>still</u> aren't built or optimized for mobile use; and even the most conscientious webmasters can't really keep the data on these sites current because everything is changing way too fast. High velocity computing can rapidly supply the framework and the appropriate context for delivery, but that's not the same as effectively generating authentic and engaging content as opposed to rote and routine responses. And very frankly, adding a couple of widgets, a sidecar Twitter feed, or a few other flashy bells and whistles doesn't contribute anything much to the utility equation or to the perceived value of a visit. Too often searching the web these days is an exhausting and unproductive waste of time unless you know precisely what you're looking for.

And things aren't ever going to get better because all the positive movement and all the vectors are pointing in the wrong direction for anyone to even imagine a day when websites will once again matter. Mobile online use has convincingly overtaken the desktop and the usage gap is growing every quarter across all cohorts and age groups. In addition, and most strikingly, over 80% of the current mobile online use is now channeled <u>opaquely</u> through applications rather than overtly and transparently through browsers. This migration to mobile applications (and the closed-off connection conduits that they create) have created what I call the "App Gap" for Google because you can't measure and you certainly can't monetize what you can't see.

And the rapidly widening social gap is even more problematic for Google. The vast volume of meaningful traffic, the influential action and engaged activity, and ALL of the buzz and energy are focused today on social actions and sharing and not on search or research. Search is a sporadic, need-based and linear process. When it's done in the moment, it's done. Social is an emotional, expansive and ongoing sharing experience which is not only contagious, but exponential in that it grows and builds on itself. As a rule of thumb, and at least until you get burned or reach a certain age, the more you share, the more you're inclined to share in the future because you become increasingly psychologically invested in the process. Information may want to be free, but it turns out (no surprise here) that we want to be with our friends. There are a number of complex and powerful drivers behind these group and cohort-based behavioral changes, but one thing is abundantly clear – none of this is good news for Google.

As the novelty of "search" has worn off and the pure excitement of spontaneous exploration has dissipated, search has changed from a joy to just a job. It's an incidental and reflexive part of our day and nothing more. The more efficient and informed that search became; the less interesting and serendipitous it was. It was the triumph of the dispassionate engineers – all about dispatch and discipline (speed and results) with all the drama and passion of discovery being drained away. In a sense, Google did its job too well.

Today search is a heavily-manipulated mirror (reflecting back and confirming what we already know) rather than a window on new worlds. Among other critical differences from the much more intriguing Facebook interest graph approach is that in order to launch a Google search, you pretty much have to know where you're headed and you need create at least a modestly informed description of what you're looking for. The search box doesn't fill itself. It's not an adventure; it's a task. It's not a place we want to go these days; it's a place where we have to go when we need to accomplish some narrow and specific inquiry. The web today is about work, not wonder. And it's lonely out there as well because search is a solitary enterprise and we're all social animals.

The App Gap is just Google's latest problem as it struggles to continue to matter in a marketplace where the playing field has changed radically while Google's core offerings really haven't. Google needs to find a way into these new activity spaces, but many of its belated and reactive responses (and even its new and somewhat novel offerings) have fallen way short of the mark. Google was great when the web was about links, pages and anonymity. But when Facebook made it personal and the smart phone made it social and mobile, Google simply lost its way. You can't engineer emotions and you can't arbitrarily construct connections and engagement with others.

Shopping and social are where it's at today and, in those sectors, Google's become an also-ran. Maybe not quite as much of a yawn as Yahoo, but nothing to write home about for sure. Far more people search every day for products on Amazon than on Google even though its new Product Listing Ads (PLAs) are arguably better suited to mobile search than Amazon's offerings. The problem is no one knows they're there because no one sees them. And why is that? Because search isn't sexy or exciting any more. If there's one thing worse than being a chore or a commodity, it's being a tool or a utility. And the situation in the social sphere is even worse. Google+ has plenty of what I would characterize as "manufactured" members, but they're generally ghosts and they're not engaged with the service and – worst of all - they're simply not sharing. G+ has about 2% of the social sharing activity today while Facebook has over 50%, Twitter is at about 24% and LinkedIn and Pinterest account for another 19%.

If you don't have a substantial seat at the table, it's hard to have anything meaningful to say about the game or to the players. Without a window into Facebook's world; some perspective on Pinterest; or any idea of what's happening on Instagram, Twitter or WhatsApp, it feels like Google's on the outside looking in and you have to wonder how much longer Google's advertising model will make sense to the major media and advertising buyers. If you're not where your advertisers' targets are spending their time and money, at the end of the day, you're nowhere.

SIMPLY STREAMING ... SUCKS

Please stop streaming stuff that sucks. No one cares. No one's watching. And, just because you can do it doesn't mean you should. And, as hard as it is to imagine, just because it happened to you doesn't make it interesting to us. You're constantly cluttering up the channels with your crap. And it seems like the spread of cheap video tools and technology isn't helping the situation – it's actually making it worse because now every clown with a camera can be a digital media publisher. Technology used without talent is less than a tool – it's a tragedy.

And even new innovations like *Hyperlapse* compression video which can speed up and smooth out the video viewing (without the shakes and constant jumping around) can't fix the presentation problem because when we're watching speakers (as opposed to road trips), there's no way to accelerate the accompanying (and obviously necessary) audio without sounding like Mickey Mouse. Media (or technology) that gets in the way of communication is less than useless.

UGC used to mean User Generated Content which contained – at least occasionally – some useful, meaningful and authentic material. Now, as far as the glut of webcasts which are indiscriminately spewing out massive amounts of video (and, frankly, podcasts aren't typically much better), it pretty much means Unwatchable Gratuitous Claptrap.

But it doesn't have to be that way if the makers would only take a few minutes (that's all anyone has anyway) to put themselves in the viewer's shoes. If we need help sleeping or want to be bored to death, there's always

C-SPAN. And, as trite as it seems, we really do prefer quality over quantity - especially when you're asking us to commit our scarce time and – even more importantly – our attention to your offerings. It's not a volume game; it's not supposed to be a Friskies buffet; it's all about choice and value.

So next time you're getting ready to stream a talk or a panel or any other event, do us all a big favor and do these four critical things:

(1) Get a producer/director

A stream is NOT a show. Get a real producer/director (not a camera man or worse yet a tripod) who actually knows that not everything that everyone does or says during a program is worth capturing for posterity and who also knows the difference and can make intelligent choices. Get a second camera and a switcher and also (if there are slides or other presentation materials) get clean, legible digital copies of those materials as well. Incorporate the audience into the shoot. Make the visuals interesting and not static and use the zoom so we don't feel throughout the show that we got some of the worst seats in the house.

(2) Get an editor

The real value of these kinds of video-captured events isn't the few people who watch for a few minutes simultaneously online. They will generally get bored or go blind fairly quickly and bail out. If there's any lasting and archival value, it's in what use you make of the content after the fact. And to create intelligent, informative and useful content that someone will be willing to watch, you need an editor who knows the material, understands the goals, and can turn out the kind of product that you and your organization can be proud of. Vary the camera angles, intercut the slides, add some audience reactions, etc. It's not hard – it just takes some time and some thought. And it's a real talent also – not just something that people learn how to do. As Liz Taylor's 7th husband said: "I know what to do, but the challenge is to make it interesting."

(3) Give us the good stuff

Let the editor do his or her job. Cherry picking has gotten a bad name somehow, but we don't care to watch introductions that we can read, administrative announcements for the room (and we don't have to silence our cell phones), sponsor acknowledgments, or coming events calendars. Do you see where I'm going with this? Cut the crap and give us the beef – the good stuff – the 10% of the conversations that matters and from which we can learn something new. Content ultimately is cheap; wisdom is invaluable and worth watching.

(4) Give us a break

15 minutes of anything today is a lifetime. We're starting to see 7 second commercials for a reason. So decide early on what the outside time limit of your piece is going to be and then hold your editor to delivering the best material he can within those constraints. The best people will tell you that constraints encourage more creativity rather than the opposite as you might think. Think highlights and high value rather than heavy lifting. And respect the target audience's time above all.

When the dust settles, you want to be sending out something that people will want to see. Don't let your media get in the way of your message.

METRICS MATTER MORE THAN MOONSHOTS

Today, we have a much better and clearer view of where technology will take us over the next few years and how it will continue to significantly alter our lives. The primary focus – per my own personal crystal ball – will be on "efficacy" – products, services, systems, software and things that help us get other things done – more quickly and more economically. The overwhelming emphasis will be on saving us time, saving us money and making us more productive – these are the metrics that make for businesses that will consistently make their builders money as long as they continue to deliver the goods. Moonshots (literal or figurative) don't really matter in the Midwest – concrete results do.

I realize that simply shutting down the spam-spewing email systems of the world would make us all more effective, but I don't see that happening. I also don't expect to see many bionic anythings and I think we'll also have to wait quite a while for social robots and other intelligent household helpers. In fact, I wouldn't expect any dramatic advances or new "miracles" any time soon because the upcoming changes will most likely be both much more mundane and also tremendously more beneficial in ways that really matter to us. The next several generations of high-tech advances won't be about inventing new things - they will be about making the everyday objects we deal with in our day-to-day lives smarter, more responsive, and more helpful to us.

These developments will be driven by two (now fairly obvious) considerations: (1) every one of us is constantly connected to the Internet cloud by increasingly intelligent devices which will all compute; and (2) our basic expectations (which are forever growing and expanding) are that we will use these connected devices to provide us with what we need, when we need it, wherever we are, and without asking. This is the new world which we will come to call the Internet of Everything.

We'll make smarter choices every day about a wide variety of things based on vast quantities of better information which will be available all of the time in the palm of our hands. And many of the basic decisions which are required will be made quickly and automatically for us by high-velocity computers living somewhere in the cloud based on the unimaginable quantities of data being generated by every action we take, every move that we make, every venue we enter, and the trails of digital exhaust that we will leave behind wherever we go.

So what exactly are the kinds of things that we can reasonably expect to see today or in the near future? Things that will seem super cool tomorrow and which, by next year, we'll all take completely for granted.

Here are 3 categories of intelligent device-driven interactions that will become everyday parts of our lives.

(1) Who Are You Lookin' At?

The new Samsung phones turn off their screens when we aren't looking at them. New photo apps won't snap a picture if we're not smiling. Others won't take the shot until we signal them by making a fist. Our slabs and tabs are looking at us just as intently as we continue to study them.

(2) Who Are You Talkin' To?

New cloud-connected pill bottles will remind us to take our medications and just how much of each prescription we should be taking. New haptic utensils and clothes will vibrate to remind us to slow down when we're eating too fast and speed up when we're walking too slowly.

(3) <u>What Are You Waitin' For?</u>

Our phones (which we call mobile "trackers" that just happen to make calls) will alert merchants as we enter their stores to send us immediate, totally-personalized offers, specials and coupons on the way <u>into the store</u> when they're useful instead of wasting paper and trees printing long receipts that never even make it out of the grocery bags once we leave.

There are many more examples and these are just brief glimpses of the future. Exciting, challenging, and constantly changing. Buckle up.

WATCHING THE WATCH MOVE FROM NOVELTY TO NUISANCE

It's surprising how long it takes for even those of us who think we're fairly astute and self-aware to realize and acknowledge certain things in our lives and behaviors that, in retrospect and with the benefit of hindsight, seem frightfully obvious. I don't want to appear to be piling on here, but I have to admit that I've put my Apple Watch aside for now because – in a ridiculously short amount of time – the novelty wore off and it turned from what I thought might become a necessity into a nuisance. I've already got plenty of those in my life (along with a bunch of nightly chores and things I've already got to plug in and attend to) so taking on another chore and another device wasn't high on my list. And I know I'm not alone.

I'm convinced that my personal reaction isn't unique and that it's actually part of an increasingly common consumption pattern. I think we need to find a new term to describe this recurring phenomenon because it's only going to become more and more prevalent. The truth is that I've been talking about the problem for a couple of years now and, more specifically, the risks it poses to new businesses trying to introduce new products and services.

Early adopters turn out to be even more rapid rejecters. If we're fairly quick these days to adopt and try new things; the big recent change in our behaviors is that we're far more unforgiving and demanding and that we're dumping things that just don't cut it at an even faster rate. The abandonment curve is probably 10 times steeper than the adoption curve on new products. You've got to get it right - right away - because the world doesn't wait and you rarely, if ever, get a second chance or bite at the apple. The foolish fad of MVPs is over – trying to release a half-baked product to a voracious, but highly critical and choosy marketplace is simply suicide.

Maybe it's all about living in a world where we've come to expect instant gratification in all things, but I think it goes deeper than that. I think that, if you're going to try to launch a new product these days, even if you have the best designers and marketers in the world, you need to take a longer look at how we live these days and the 5 major dimensions/distractions of our daily lives and build those considerations into your offerings and your launch plan. If your offerings aren't properly aligned and consistent with how we behave and/or if you haven't developed a plan and a strategy to address each of these areas and potentially help change the underlying behaviors, your product will quickly move from smart to superfluous. In today's social world, you can fly from being the "belle of the ball" to being the "butt" of late night jokes in a flash.

In addition, once you do launch, you better have a team set and ready to help you authentically manage (yes I realize that's somewhat of an oxymoron) the word of mouth and the inevitable and highly-opinionated conversations that are sure to follow. There are no vacuums left in today's world of social media which means that, if you're not talking about your products and driving the discussion as much as possible, someone else will be.

We talk about free will, but the truth of the matter is that we are all creatures and captives of our habits. And our days are dictated to a far greater degree than we understand by the 5 C's: conversations, conventions, comparisons, compromises and chores. Think of these as multi-dimensional descriptors – some are more like scales, some are buckets of conclusions, some are expressions and choices, and some are points of reference and departure.

As you try to make sense of where the Watch is headed, and as you plan the introduction and rollout of your own new products or services, watch out for these early indicators:

Conversations

As surprising as it may be in this "all-talk, all-the-time" world, we still learn the most by listening (not talking) and a large part of everyone's day is consumed by conversations. In the old days, conversations were largely consensual and two-way deals. Today, not so much. There have always been braggarts, blowhards and bullies, but today it seems that everyone's their own outbound broadcaster (regardless of whether they have anything important to say) and opinions, not necessarily facts, are omnipresent whether we've asked for them or not.

We're trapped in this awful place between TMI (tiresome) and TMZ (tawdry or worse), but the aggregate direction of the conversation's flow is still important and instructive and the talk about the Watch is already shifting in tone from high-energy advocacy and endorsements ("Can't live without it") to more moderate and measured discussions about value and utility. From religious fervor to reasonable analysis is never the way you want the talk about your "gee-whiz" product to progress. It's a slippery slope and the Watch is already headed in the wrong direction. Just listen to the folks talking on the train.

Conventions

We're not exactly all sheep or lemmings, but we do still love to follow the crowd and the standard conventions in most things. We don't always color within the lines, but no one's rushing to jump off a cliff every day either. And, very often, the entire compliance process is so internalized and unconscious that we don't even realize what's going on. You may imagine that your new watch is going to be a great messaging device, but the guy sitting opposite you in the meeting thinks you're an impatient and inattentive asshole who keeps looking at his watch and wishing that the meeting can't be over soon enough. Not exactly the message you want to be sending to that important client or customer.

If you're old enough, you'll recall that a certain President named Bush not too many years ago probably lost an entire Presidential debate because he got caught sneaking a peek at his watch instead of paying attention to the discussion. The message was clear – he wanted badly to be somewhere else –

and the millions of people watching on TV felt that he was disconnected and that they were being dissed. It's almost the same exact problem for younger employees who try to be conscientious and take their meeting notes on their phones while the elders in the room see them and think they're insufferable idiots who are checking their email and newsfeeds instead of focusing on the matters at hand.

And then there's the basic question of who wants or needs to wear a watch anyway these days? Certainly no one under 30. We're completely surrounded by digital devices and the time is everywhere. Telling the world to take two steps backwards to re-adopt a device that was once essential, but which is now largely extraneous, makes no sense at all.

Comparisons

We generally like to proceed from the familiar and not stray too far from the tried and true in our decisions – especially about new devices and technologies. And we never want to be the guy testing the depth of the puddle by jumping in with both feet since that puddle might just be a sewer or a well. The way we manage this process day by day is by constantly performing mental comparisons – how much is something new basically the same and how much does it differ? How big a leap of faith will the transition require and how deep is the chasm? And ultimately – and most of all – are the differences actually improvements which are worth the price of change, the costs of acquisition, the pain of the mistakes due to trial and error, and the time spent on new training and learning curves?

We are all realistic enough to know that there's no free lunch and that no new products are pain free. So we look at what we are doing and using now and how well our current tools and technologies serve our needs and then we compare the new products or services to the old ways of doing whatever. In the overall scheme of things, it's hard to say that the Watch brings much new to the party. It's a lot less clunky. It's got a bevy of nice and expensive bands. It's got most of the same apps as my phone, but only a few that have already been successfully transitioned to mini-mobile use. And not much more to set it apart for half a dozen other devices.

But really the worst sign of all is that we're engaged in measuring and comparing at all. The best and most compelling products never even get this kind of a down-and-dirty review and product proctology. They're a passion, not a process. You take them on faith. And that's the kind of connection that you can also take to the bank.

Compromises

Our lives are all about choices and compromises (very few things are perfect on Day One) and we make these coin flips every day. Unfortunately, the lion's share of them are rarely between diamonds and rubies and very often they're "either/or" selections between bad and worse. So when we do have something to say about these decisions, the analysis often goes like this: (a) is it going to save me time; (b) is it going to save me money; or (c) will it make me smarter or more productive? And, more recently, will it increase my status?

We're willing to make deals every day, and we're willing to invest some time and effort in making things happen, but we have to believe that there's some actual value in each transaction to make it worth our while. When you run the Watch through this calculus, it's hard to make much of an argument in its favor. So when you apply the traditional tests (time, money, and productivity), there's not a lot to hang your hat on and absolutely nothing that your phone alone won't pretty much do for you already. Ask yourself what it really buys you to have your watch tell you to take your phone out of your pocket so you can do something. And when you get to questions around status, all I can say is Glass. Just remind yourself how quickly the Google Glass went from cool to creepy to compost. It's just a matter of time before people will start to check out your Watch and quietly wonder if you didn't get the memo.

Chores

We're all beyond busy these days and things aren't gonna get better any time soon so the last thing we need is more unnecessary assignments and chores. Keeping our critical devices charged up is enough of a hassle as it is and worrying every night about your Watch as well is just too much. And I'm pretty sure that having my phone ping my Watch all day long over Bluetooth is sucking the juice more quickly out of my phone as well. And don't get me started on the question of what kind of fitness monitor the thing can be when it's sitting on your desk charging for a few hours instead of being on your wrist keeping score. I've written about battery failure and Fitbit anxiety before. See http://www.inc.com/howard-tullman/fitbit-anxiety-is-part-of-a-larger-problem.html. But until someone really makes an 18 hour watch battery, I'm just not a believer.

So that's my take. These are just my humble opinions. And while I may be lonely for a while –just you watch – I won't be alone for long.

NEVER TRY TO BOIL THE OCEAN

As many times as I remind people that it's always a bad bet for any company to try to be all things to all people unless you have the technology to support mass customization solutions (See http://www.inc.com/howard-tullman/surprise-you-can-be-all-things-to-all-people.html) and that, in the vast majority of cases, this scattered and over-extended approach results in a business that's spread a mile wide and an inch deep; I'm still confronted almost every day with new examples of the same problem. No one gets anything 100% right the first time out and trying to build a product or service that is so comprehensive that it works for the world is crazy. I'm still confronted almost every day with new examples of the same problem.

This isn't a problem that's limited to new or small businesses with little or no experience. The biggest guys in the business are equally adept at repeatedly stubbing their toes in exactly the same way – they try to boil the whole ocean by biting off too much too soon and trying to address every possible part of every market and they quickly end up choking in the process. Niches are nice and a really smart place to focus as you start.

You would think that anyone with any smarts (or at least some access to any decent tech conference or publication in the last decade) would be sick of hearing and absolutely know by now that a lack of early focus (or an inability to say "no" on a regular basis to ideas that are clearly attractive, but off target) is a certain formula for failure. You can try to do pretty much anything you want today, but you can't do it all at once. This isn't new news.

I've been harping on this subject myself for 20 years or more. Focus, focus and more focus – start small, nail it, then scale it.

The fact is that, when Henry Ford launched the Model T, I'm reasonably sure that the last things on his mind were seat coverings, trim options or paint colors. You could buy your new Ford automobile in any color that you wanted as long as it was basic black. He knew that he had much bigger fish to fry – matters of substance, not style – if he was going to ultimately succeed in a cost-effective manner on a large scale. So he focused on the big things first. The new car was all about function, not fashion, and it was also an early lesson for all of us on the importance of laser-like focus and tunnel-vision when you're launching not just a new product, but new ideas, categories and behaviors as well.

At the same time, as everyone knows, had he been too focused on simply incremental improvements (faster horses), he would have never made the critical jump over the chasm and into the future. See http://www.inc.com/howard-tullman/stop-focusing-see-around-corners-instead.html . So a little balance and some perspective are big advantages also.

Apple used to have the same kind of courage of its convictions in its new products - at least while Steve Jobs was still alive. Ear buds for the iPad – you can have any shade of white that you like. Model selection across several products - meager or non-existent or pre-packed at the factory. Consumer choices – not really interested. The whole marketing posture sent a clear message to the consumer that Apple had already made all the important choices for you and they'd tell you what to like. Frankly, as cool and stylish as the products were, what was really critical was what was under the cover and inside the box. In the end, that's what really matters.

White pretty much used to be for Apple what Black was to the Model T. In fact, you could argue that the eventual advent of a variety of colors at Apple (black, white and silver don't count) for the 5c as an example along with the proliferation of a dozen bands for the new Watch weren't triumphs of innovation or new ideas; they were basically fairly confusing and boring line extensions which were more reflections of just a touch of desperation rather than design. The only thing we know for sure these days is that hesitating and hedging your bets as well as halfway execution aren't the hallmarks of any great entrepreneurs.

Today it feels a lot like what was really lost when Steve died was that singular sense of unerring confidence which I thought of as his "sometimes wrong, but never in doubt" approach. A little hubris isn't exactly the worst thing an entrepreneur can have when he or she is first starting out – it's probably critical. Apple used to be all about an intensely focused effort to do a very few elegant things really well. The feeling seemed to be "we'll always be Apple and never be Android". In fact, Apple still brags about all of its products fitting on the kitchen table, but - to me - the burgeoning product mix these days looks more like potpourri than perfection.

And guess, on the other hand, who seems to have learned its lesson and who's getting it right these days? At least as to Glass. It's Google that's taking a couple of steps backwards in order to move the whole wearable computing category forward. They're doing it by (a) narrowing their focus (not chasing the consumer for now); (b) addressing a limited number of problem sets; and (c) going after target customer markets with readily-discoverable best use cases and the most obvious and low-hanging solutions. It's all about industrial uses and enterprise level solutions for now rather than trying to continue to change the behavior of consumers across the entire planet overnight.

It seemed pretty obvious to me from Day One that Glass was a perfect tool for the surgical suite (photos, narration, shared viewing, largely hands-free and sterile, etc.) and a farce for the fashionistas. And if they get it right with Glass, you can bet that we're going to see a very similar strategy with respect to Google voice search and voice recognition in general (even Siri) which has suffered for decades from the same attempts to overreach instead of focusing on the immediate opportunities to massively increase industry productivity by addressing easy needs rather than beating their heads against the wall trying to solve the last 1% of the problem.

Voice recognition is essentially more than 100% accurate when it is properly employed to interpret, capture and respond to a fixed and basic vocabulary and/or a finite set of commands. This is why it will be so central to the next several generations of the connected car where we'll never see a keyboard that makes any sense. And the opportunities are huge because millions of businesses have exactly these kinds of finite vocabularies of products, services, descriptions and conditions or instructions which could use accurate voice control systems every day to save millions of man hours which are now wasted with inventory functions, clipboards, scanning guns, etc.

The introduction of new technology is always tough and the obvious conclusion is that you don't have to make it harder than necessary on yourself by aiming too high at the outset. Focusing on immediate problem solving for customers who are willing, able and interested in buying what you've got to sell today is the name of the game.

PART III

MAVENS, MENTORS AND MASTERS OF THE UNIVERSE IN THE DIGITAL AGE

WHEN YOU COME TO
THE FORK, TAKE IT

We've been told practically since birth that a lot of the success we hope for in business (and in life) will come from being a good listener and from being <u>really</u> good at following directions. Consistency is another highly regarded and very traditional virtue along with learning from our experiences. But what if - in a world driven and dominated by technology that is changing much faster than ever before and picking up more speed every day – all of this conventional wisdom was basically wrong?

What if past experience wasn't your best friend, but your worst enemy because it was no longer predictive of virtually anything and, worse yet, because it was actually an impediment to the kinds of disruptive change and innovation that we need today to remain competitive and ultimately to lead the global pack? Letting go of what has worked for you in the past isn't ever easy, but it's ever more critical that these kinds of questions be a significant part of the decision set.

What if being consistent wasn't the smart thing to do (that is – to keep doing things the way you had always done them), but was actually fairly stupid in that it meant that - in the months and years that had intervened since you initially made a plan and started executing it – you hadn't learned anything that required changes, updates, pivots or even dropping whole lines of unproductive or unprofitable business? As Emerson said, "a foolish consistency is the hobgoblin of little minds." And frankly, who really needs more hobgoblins – whatever they are?

I'm especially concerned these days about a different kind of directions (in the compass sense of the word (North or South – to or from) rather than meaning "instructions") and how important it is going to be for all of us to understand and appreciate the ways in which the flows of critical information, assets and resources have reversed their directions/polarities over the last few years so that we can quickly adapt our businesses and our operations to address the new and very different requirements that these changes dictate. And to understand the necessary changes, we're going to need some very smart people and some strong compasses (rather than historical road maps which aren't worth much these days) to help us find our way.

What's the absolutely simplest example? The obvious fact that ubiquitous connectivity, information sharing and universal access have turned every form of publication, broadcast and communication (formerly one-way or one-to-many) into a bi-directional or multi-directional conversation (at least two-way or more). The "I talk, you listen" model of anything (media, sales and marketing, education and training, and even governance) is totally toast. Everyone's an "expert"; every opinion (based on facts or factoids) registers and counts; and sadly, in many cases, the biggest blowhard beats the brightest bulb. Sheer tonnage today trumps tact and very often the truth. This situation can't last, but it's what we've got to deal with today. The goal is to find the new business opportunities and advantages hidden in the piles of gossip and garbage.

And what does the omnipresent cloud and the massive amounts of content of all kinds which now reside there tell us about the changed directions? It tells us that we're entering a world of PULL where we'll pull (and extract) information and intelligence from the cloud as and when needed and where we're in control of the information equation rather than PUSH (and swallow) where we're simply passive consumers of whatever crap is forced down the pipelines and feed to us. There's just too much noise, too much information, and too many complex and overwhelming decisions coming at us for anyone to effectively process the data and make wise choices.

But that's exactly the kind of information overload that makes for great opportunities for those companies which can help us choose, niche, filter, process and decide what makes sense for each of us. Companies that can help us find just what we're looking for (and no more) will set the standards for search in the future because "knowing" is going to be an insurmountable task for anyone whereas "knowing where to look" to find the answers will be the new name of the game. Chicago-based SimpleRelevance (www. simplerelevance.com) is a start-up developing and providing cost-effective analytical tools for the "rest of us" to make smart choices and sense out of masses of available (but not necessarily readily accessible) data in a cost-effective manner.

The truth is that – in virtually every commercial exchange – the information equation has been reversed because of the improved access (for better or worse) which buyers have to group intelligence, shared opinion and pricing data which were formerly held and controlled solely by sellers and the playing field for negotiations has been altered in the consumers' favor forever. And this isn't simply a matter of getting a better price on some product or selecting a smarter service provider for your lawn care.

It's clear that no industry or profession is immune to these directional shifts. Medicine offers two great examples. First, in the old days, we picked a doctor (usually through family connections or other word of mouth) and then – if necessary – the doctor told us which hospital he or she was connected with and that's where we went for our surgery or other procedures. There was no choice, no shopping around, no arguing – just "doctor's orders". In the near future, that order will be completely reversed for the vast majority of patients in America. We will pick or be assigned a health services organization and that company will specify and dictate our hospital, our doctor, and even to a very large extent our course of treatment or non-treatment. Accountants and clerks we've never met will decide whether we "need" (and their companies will pay for) certain tests and medication rather than our doctors.

And if these changes didn't make our doctors feel somewhat diminished (to say the least), just think about how drug advertising has changed the game and turned them into glorified waiters and order takers. In the grand old days, if we were sick and saw our doctor, he prescribed any necessary medications. In fact, that ability – to write scripts - was the defining legal characteristic of being a doctor. Today, thanks to TV and the web, we go into the doctor's office and tell him that we need the "purple pill" or a Z-pack and we won't take "no" for an answer because we saw it on TV and now we're the experts. Talk about TMI. And, as a result, the doctors spend their days arguing with us about ads we've seen on the tube rather than telling us what we need (or very often) or don't need for our problems. And if we don't like their answer or their reluctance to give us what we think we need, increasingly, we can go to see a nurse practitioner or clerk at our neighborhood drug store and get our fix right there.

As the information around us expands and implodes at the same time, and we are all swamped in the unceasing flow of data and TMI, we're looking at another major inflection point (or - as Yogi Berra would say – another fork in the road) and, while it's not very clear what lies on the path ahead, it's obvious that if we don't make some hard choices and just stand still, we'll be run over. Where you head is less important today than the fact that you keep moving and head somewhere. When you get to the fork in the road, take it.

SHUT UP AND LISTEN – YOU MIGHT JUST LEARN SOMETHING

One of the most interesting parts of my job at 1871 is listening to our member companies. For most entrepreneurs, effective and patient listening is a fairly foreign concept. They think that the opposite of talking isn't listening; it's waiting to talk. Partially this is because they think that they have to always be selling and they're always trying to fill any dead air and suck all the oxygen out of the room. But sometimes, you just need to catch your breath and let the other guy have his say. As it happens, bits of actual wisdom are the rewards you often get for listening when you would have preferred to speak.

These days, I think that listening is a rare and highly undervalued skill. It's an area in which every one of us could use some improvement and developing good listening skills can make a world of difference for your business and in your leadership. Listening carefully is the highest form of courtesy and professionalism. As my Mother used to say: "this is why God gave us two ears and only one mouth." If I had only listened back then, there's no telling where I'd be today.

So every day I get to hear as much and as many of the trials and tribulations of the hundreds of entrepreneurs who work here at startup central as I can stand. I try to be patient and objective as long as they have taken the time: (1) to do their homework and get prepared; (2) to organize their thoughts and their questions; and (3) to specifically identify the areas where they think I can help or at least advise them. Folks who just drop by to shoot the breeze quickly find themselves shooting it somewhere else with someone else.

If they're not prepared and if they have that little respect for my time; it's hard to imagine that they would really care about my thoughts and opinions or that I should waste my relatively scarce time sharing my reactions with them. I think this is a very fair expectation on both sides of the discussion – whether you're the "oldie" or the "newbie" in any conversation; you need to bring it or don't bother coming.

And, of course in the course of the conversations, generally when I'm asked, and often whether or not I'm asked, I'm not especially shy (and rarely polite) about giving them my impressions and the alleged benefit of my years of experience which may occasionally keep them from making the same mistakes that I made in similar circumstances. Sometimes, I discover that they're trying to create solutions before they've spent enough time listening to their customers' problems which is a lot like working in the dark. Other times I find that just the act of having someone seriously listening to them (who doesn't have an attitude, an interest or an agenda) does wonders for their mental health and their anxiety levels. But that's not to say that I think that these skull sessions should be warm and fuzzy chats.

I like to save the "strokes" for their co-workers, friends and families. Honestly, I'd rather be fair and frank than spend my time beating around the bush and worrying more about their feelings than their future. My process is aggressive and unapologetic – I'm trying to make them and their businesses better – that's all there is to it. It's never about me. But it does have a lot to do with argument and challenge – pressing and pushing them to think about the tough issues and the non-obvious answers - rather than supplying their standard responses. I want to make sure that they have the courage of their convictions and the willingness to stick by their guns. We often describe this posture as "sometimes wrong, but never in doubt."

That's because you need a thick skin to succeed in this crazy startup business and the internal and external calluses which will ultimately come to protect you are developed and grow strong in the crucible of confrontation (and hard questions) and not in courteous conversations steeped in superficial compliments. Some babies are just ugly – and some ideas just suck. It always helps to tell it like it is and the truth only hurts when it should.

Having said all that, I'd still certainly rather have them not just listen to my advice, but take it as well. I do vehemently believe that great serial entrepreneurs are masters in pattern recognition and – in the startup space – there are very, very few problems and very little else that represent truly new issues or – as the courts say – cases of first impression. In 95% of the situations, for better or worse, these are "movies" that I've seen before. Everyone I know and those I speak to about this who have made it their life's work to consistently light up new businesses will tell you that – while you're always gonna make new mistakes – the real key to succeeding more often than you fail is to avoid making the same mistakes over and over again.

I can't speak for the many guys who've been successful once in this business of new businesses – I'm sure that even they aren't sure whether they were terribly smart or terrifically lucky or, most likely, a bunch of both. It's never really that clear whether their particular success was mainly due to a good idea, good partners, good timing or simple good luck – not that there's anything wrong with any of these elements. I like to say: "Just because you've done it once doesn't make you Jesus."

And I've written before about marginal mentors (http://www.inc.com/howard-tullman/how-to-deal-with-marginal-mentors.html) and on the subject of how little having made or accumulated a lot of money has to do with having the mental horsepower and the chops to help someone drag his business out of a ditch. Money doesn't really care who makes it and having a lot of money – as we all know from experience – clearly doesn't make you wise.

But for those of us who have lived through the very prolonged and painful process of successfully birthing businesses over and over again, it all comes down to listening and paying attention. And to one more important thing: the winners are those who learn to listen patiently without losing either their self-confidence or their temper.

DO MARGINAL MENTORS
REALLY MATTER?

I'm fairly certain that there's an overabundance of highly-verbal and successful people who are flattered to be asked and more than willing and even excited about the prospect of giving sporadic advice to young entrepreneurs. I say "sporadic" because - even in the best and most structured and organized incubators, accelerators and other start-up and tune-up support facilities - the mentoring process has a lot of hit and miss qualities. People drop by for an hour or two – rarely actually up-to-speed on the business in question or the critical issues on the table – and then they listen briefly to the entrepreneurs, nod sagely, take their best shot at some quick suggestions and advice and then leave. And sadly, the next guy dropping in to meet with that same team might have identical or completely opposite advice.

It's no doubt a learning experience for the entrepreneurs, but I'm not really sure what they're learning or gaining from the process. I believe that when you take the time to give someone advice (and you take their time as well), you're obligated to do what you can (in terms of preparation, connections, referrals, etc.) to make sure that it's not just lip service or a bunch of empty clichés.

Some of these "advisors" are one-hit wonders themselves and it's not really that clear whether their particular success was mainly due to a good idea, good partners, good timing or simple good luck – not that there's anything wrong with any of these elements – and I'd rather be blessed in any business with all of the above if I had a choice. But you have to wonder – as you're listening to their war stories – exactly how much transferable wisdom they've gained from the experience and, more specifically, how much they've extracted and generalized from their situation which will be of use and value to your own business.

Giving advice is a form of high-minded, self-congratulatory nostalgia for these folks in many respects and, in addition, it's frightfully easy in these situations to tell someone else what to do because nothing is impossible for the person who doesn't have to do it himself. What's more, a lot of these people will tell you to take a hard line on something and stand up on principle until push comes to shove and then they're long gone. I like to say that a principle really isn't a principle until it costs you something.

Another aspect of the process that's somewhat problematic is the matter of money. Money doesn't care who makes it and having a lot of money – as we all know from experience – doesn't really make you wise or make you a class act. And I realize that rich entrepreneurs sometimes complain that when you have money, people tend to doubt your talent. But in many cases that's exactly the fact. And, for me, it's really hard to pay a lot of attention to the advice of someone with no skin in the game. I like people who put their money where their mouth is. My favorite trader (I realize that's somewhat of an oxymoron) likes to say that "until you have a position, all you have is an opinion" and I agree.

Any entrepreneur's time is precious and constrained – if you're going to spend it listening to anyone for any substantial amount of time, make sure (as best you can) that they know what they're talking about and that the conversations are worth your time.

Here are a couple of thoughts to help you through the process.

(1) As Simon and Garfunkel said so well in *The Boxer:* "…a man hears what he wants to hear/and disregards the rest". Listen carefully, weigh everything with a grain of salt, and try to determine why the person would (or should) know what they're talking about. Then take the best and leave the rest.

(2) If the person is also a prospective investor in your business (and one that you think you'd like to have and could live with), remember that listening to advice very often accomplishes far more than actually heeding it. Be patient, nod your head a lot, agree with their observations, and then go on and do what you think is best for the business. Frankly, I think in crazy times like these, lying probably gets more businesses started than money.

(3) Try to remember that personality and rapport are not substitutes for credibility and knowledge. They make for pleasant conversations, but just because someone's a really good guy only rarely also means that he knows what he's talking about. These are people you'd happily buy a drink for, but never lend any money.

And finally, keep in mind the strange paradox that there are people who can give you extremely useful and valuable information and direction, but who can't get out of their own way in their own businesses and who would be the first to admit that they really don't do a good job of taking their own advice. Don't follow their example, but listen to their suggestions.

SHOULD EVERY "EXPERT" COMES WITH AN EXPIRATION DATE

These days, for better or worse, professed experts in every conceivable area of business are a dime a dozen and, in most cases, I'd say that they (and their alleged expertise and invaluable advice) are worth just about that much. And, in all events, they are clearly worth considerably less than you'd spend on a good cup of coffee. And just like spoiled cream can kill a great cup of java; out-of-date ideas from people who the developments in new technologies have clearly passed by should be date-stamped with the understanding that their time has come and gone and that they're no longer worth listening to – politely or otherwise.

It seems that everyone claims to be an expert on something today and they're shameless and more than happy to sell you (and everyone you know) their various services for a tidy sum. Some of these people are one-hit wonders trying to re-invent themselves and it's not clear whether their prior "success" was mainly due to a good idea, good partners, good timing or simple good luck. So you have to wonder – as you're listening to their war stories – exactly how much transferable wisdom they've gained from their own experiences and how much of that knowledge will be of use and value to your own business.

And, just like cigarettes, I think a lot of these characters ought to come with a large warning label (maybe something like "take this advice with as many large grains of salt as possible") because – in addition to wasting your time and money – these people can be clearly be harmful to your business.

And their misdirected guidance can take years off your life - just like a pack-a-day smoking habit. In today's high-velocity and hyper-competitive markets; speed kills (in a good way) if it's you that's moving down the road. But if you're heading in the wrong direction because you listened to the wrong advice; you could find yourself way behind the curve and trying to play catch-up with your competition.

Now, I'm sure there are always valuable things to be learned from others and that - within their own experience base and their given areas of expertise – there really are experts who can add value to your strategy and your business if their input is timely and current. But it's not easy to separate the wheat from the chaff or to figure out who can really give you a helping hand and your money's worth. Your time is a scarce and precious resource and it's always constrained. If you're going to spend it listening to anyone for any substantial amount of time, make sure (as best you can) that they know what they're talking about and that the conversations are worth it.

I think that there are a few guidelines and ideas to keep in mind when you find yourself having to evaluate situations like this.

(1) Process Experts Have a Longer Shelf Life than Domain Experts

A domain expert knows a lot about what to do in a specific area or situation and in a defined space or industry. That knowledge is the stuff that spoils quickly over time if it's not refreshed and renewed – especially with regard to new technologies. It's critical to be a life-long and continual learner. A process expert knows how to repeatedly do things effectively in whatever situation or industry you happen to be in. Successful serial entrepreneurs call this skill "pattern recognition" and it means simply that many situations present problems that aren't materially different (regardless of the specifics) from those that seasoned operators have seen and solved hundreds of times before. Guys who know the proper approaches and have mastered the change management process never go out of date.

(2) <u>An Expert's Knowledge Can Exceed His Experience But Only Rarely</u>

There's a lot of delusional mythology around the extensibility of skills and expertise. Much of this BS is promulgated by the people trying to sell you their services even when it's an obvious stretch and a complete leap of faith to believe that they can really add value based on their actual backgrounds and experience. Even the most successful players need to know and – more importantly – admit the limits of their skill sets. You only need to recall Michael Jordan's abortive career as a professional <u>baseball</u> player to see what I'm sayin'. Lawyers (as a race) are also great at never saying "No" to doing anything regardless of their actual qualifications. They're always ready to take the fee and the assignment and then you have the privilege (and the risks) of paying for their OTJ learning curve and education. Not a smart choice – ever. You need to find the right person with the right experience and tools in the right industry (your industry) and not try to make do or accept someone saying that what they did elsewhere is easy to apply to your situation.

(3) <u>Knowledge is Subject to the Law of Diminishing Returns in Most Cases</u>

In addition to simply going stale or out of date, whatever accumulation of knowledge and expertise you may have and apply to your situation, you should understand that it can only take you so far. It's true that we are always learning, but that doesn't mean that we are necessarily getting smarter in the process. After a certain point, the facts and figures and past wisdom run out of steam and this is when the best entrepreneurs really earn their stripes and their keep. It's at the point when you need to use your best judgment; your intuition; and a little prayer (which never hurts) to get you over the last hurdle and through the woods to the finish line that you learn whether you've got what it takes to succeed. No one else can do it for you. No one else can make those last calls and choices. It's all up to you because – in the final analysis – and in the critical moments of decision – no one knows your business better than you.

(4) <u>Hire the Expert Who Can Get You There, not the One Who Says He's Been There Before</u>

In business, just as in your sex life, especially as you get older, it's important to remember that past results are no guarantee of future performance. A track record is an important and very valuable part of the evaluation process for any expert, but you're not headed backwards and your job is to make sure that the people you are planning to work with have the desire, the energy and the skills to help you move your business forward.

DEALING WITH DOOFUSES AND OTHER WASTES OF TIME

I like to think that the best entrepreneurs are masters of cutting to the chase. They're very focused, of course, but more importantly they're especially efficient because they don't really have any other choice. Scarce resources, limited time, and a regularly shrinking bank account do a whole lot for your concentration. And the non-stop streams of decisions (large and small) which they face every day are roughly like living in a batting cage with a machine firing fastball pitches at your head every 15 seconds. It means they've got to be 'on purpose" and "on point" all the time. Patience isn't exactly a virtue in this kind of frantic fast-forward environment and tolerance – especially of time-wasting doofuses – is a very rare commodity.

In addition, because entrepreneurs live in a world where they need to be constantly calculating opportunity costs, the smartest ones are always asking themselves the same two questions:

(1) Is what I'm doing right now moving us forward toward the goal; and

(2) Is what I'm doing right now the highest and best use of my time and talents?

Frankly, if you're not asking yourselves these same questions at least a couple of times a day, then your people and your business are running your life and making your choices for you instead of the other way around which is how it should be. You always want to run the business based on your outbox and not your inbox.

It's absolutely true that (starting with Steve Jobs) some of the sharpest and most effective CEOs I have known over the last 30 years might seem like arrogant, asocial and abrupt assholes to most people (and that's when they're in a good mood), but, in their hearts (or what's left of them), they're just aggressively optimizing their time and their opportunities on a continual basis and constantly assigning new priorities to things in real time. They aren't being rude or dismissive; they're just attentive to things that they regard at that moment as more important. They're doing what they think is right – right at that moment – no more, no less and no promises as to what the next moment will bring. That's just how it works.

To say that they don't suffer fools lightly is a gross understatement. The truth is that they regard most people as something between a nuisance and a necessary evil. But the fact is that we need leaders like this to make important things happen and they can't all be charming social butterflies even if they had the time which, of course, they don't. As the old saying goes: "money doesn't come from singing. It comes from work."

So it usually falls to other people in the organization to help the fiercely focused founders and CEOs figure out how to deal with the people who are simply doofuses, masters of make-work, and/or wizards of window-dressing <u>and</u> who, for better or worse (and mainly for worse), are not only necessary evils; they're generally part of the whole package that comes with your decision to accept third-party financing whether it's high-end angel investors, private equity groups or traditional venture investors.

If you take their money, you get to take all the crap that comes right along with it and you're supposed to smile at that prospect. Thank you, sir. May I have another? But, smiling or shrugging (just don't get caught sulking), every entrepreneur needs to figure out how to deal with these people because they're here to stay. It's not easy (it's a little like putting out a fire in your hair with a hammer), but it does help to understand who you're dealing with and how you can help. Frankly, anything that you can do as a senior team member to help your fiercely focused CEO manage this process and also to run interference for the rest of the folks on the team couldn't be more valuable.

First, and foremost, remember who you're going to actually be dealing with from day-to-day.

I guess there's a version of the old "bait and switch" routine in every business – the car guys may be the masters, but the VCs and PE guys aren't very far behind in the BS business. You start out talking to a guy who could buy a small country and end up working with people who can't approve a pepperoni pizza for a party without checking with personnel. It's a rude awakening and disappointing for sure – but it's just another part of the business that you need to get used to. The trick is to get the rules of engagement straight at the outset and to not let the turkeys get you down.

Second, you need to remember that these folks basically have never begun or run anything.

By and large, you'll learn that they are consumed with matters and minutia of form over substance. They worry much more about font sizes and folders than about the actual facts and figures of the business. It's all about presentations and the "process" rather than real prospects and progress. None of these guys wants to give their Emperor(s) the bad news. I call this the doctrine of "no new news is ever good news". Their absolute worst nightmare is to EVER be the bearer of changes, surprises or any bad news. They know only too well what happens to the messenger.

Third, generally the players that you're unlucky enough to get stuck with really don't have day jobs.

As far as I can tell, their main occupation (other than making work for you) is to somehow justify their own positions. They can turn the simple scheduling of meetings (the more the merrier) into major undertakings and marathons of telephone and email tag. And they think the meetings themselves are the end game and that counting meetings counts – rather than what gets done in the meetings. And it gets worse. Everything they touch has to be over-analyzed; repeatedly chewed over; and ultimately cleared with everyone including the dog in the lobby. It's a painful, time-wasting process.

Finally, I really wasn't kidding about the pizza. These people have absolutely no ultimate authority to do or approve anything (other than hiring outside consultants on your dime) without running back and clearing it with a multitude of higher-ups. The only way that you can ever lose your job at one of these investment firms is by saying "yes" to something. No one ever lost their job by saying "no" and that's not going to change in our lifetimes. So it's pretty much a waste of your time and your breath to ask these guys for anything since they can't write the check in any event. You don't want to be dealing with the monkey when the organ grinder is in the room.

So, what can you do to keep things moving forward for the business in spite of these people?

(1) You can't completely ignore them, but you can take your time in responding and this will actually save you time and effort in the long run because – as often as not – they'll never follow up and pursue many of their demands.

(2) You can do whatever you can to contain and limit their involvement (and thereby protect at least some of your team's time) by insisting on being the funnel for all their interactions with and inquiries to the team.

(3) As a test, you can initially respond to certain requests simply and quickly and then determine whether anyone is actually reading, reviewing and/or acting upon any of the submitted materials. Much of the time you'll never hear another word on the subject because it's likely that no one will even be looking at the stuff requested.

(4) But, sadly, here's the one thing you can't do: you actually can't try to go around these mini-gatekeepers in order to try to get to the real decision makers because – just like in any classic John le Carre espionage novel – it turns out that everyone on their side (top to bottom) is a part of the program and needs to preserve the fiction that their plans, processes and procedures actually make sense and work. No one, including the Emperor, wants to ever hear otherwise.

SITUATIONAL ETHICS SUCK

I'm afraid that we're developing another generation gap and this one isn't merely cosmetic (can't stand those tattoos!) or aurally aesthetic (can't stand that music!) or even extreme economic (why "own" anything). It's far more important than any of these fairly superficial differences and preferences – albeit I recognize that they are crushingly important to the hosts of *TMZ* and *Access Hollywood*.

And it's far more pressing and critical than the angst and quasi-parental concerns these weird choices engender in us grown-ups. I can deal with all the questionable choices that many young people are making today because I'm relatively sure that we all made similar (or much worse, but probably less long-lasting) choices in our youth and yet, amazingly enough, we're still here, standing tall, and giving them advice and the "benefit" of our wisdom – such as it is.

But I'm not talking about something that's a preference or an option that we can take or leave – I'm talking about a problem that threatens to undermine something so fundamental and basic to the conduct of business (and especially to early-stage angel investing) that almost everyone (other than those in the film or music business) has always taken it for gospel and for granted. They say every day in the film business, "I'll love you 'til I don't" so get used to it. But that kind of fleeting attachment or commitment and the complete absence of sincerity that's "just business" in those worlds isn't the way we hope and expect that the rest of the sane (and square) business world conducts itself.

That's why I'm getting increasingly concerned about this very basic idea. I recently heard Alan Matthew (a long-time successful options and commodities trader) express it forcefully in about 15 different ways throughout a recent talk he gave to several hundred entrepreneurs at 1871. He said that, in every deal he does, and in every transaction: "My word is my bond." And it's just that simple – especially in the trading pits in Chicago – where the entire ecosystem depends on trust and the ability for everyone to rely on the commitments and honesty of the other players. But the problem is that - even as essential a part as this attitude is to how we do business in Chicago - I don't think we're doing a good job of communicating this very critical concept to today's young entrepreneurs. Too many of them live in a different conceptual world – one driven by situational ethics. And it sucks.

Telling people half the story or what they want to hear instead of what they need to hear isn't a funding solution – it's an invitation to a later slaughter. And it's usually the entrepreneur and the management team who will ultimately get killed. So it makes sense to share ALL of the news all the time – if for no other reason than to just save yourself all the grief coming down the line. The truth never hurts unless it ought to and sometimes it's a powerful wake-up call for all concerned. There's never a really good or special time to decide to tell the truth – the time is all the time.

But, if you haven't been there (to make the right choice regardless of how hard or discouraging it may be or how it may impact your financing or prospects) and there's no one more experienced around to guide you because you're running full-speed ahead and you're also making it up as you go, it's far too easy to take a quick slide down that slippery ethical slope. And once you lose someone's confidence, once they come to believe that you don't share and abide by their fundamental values, you will never get their trust and support entirely back.

And, honestly, because a whole generation of kids have been told (at least since second grade) that they're amazing, exceptional and completely unique, it's just a short step for them to conclude that the ordinary rules don't apply to them and that morals are just for little people and that they're way above that somewhat mundane conformity and far too smart for it as well. An old friend of mine used to say – by way of excusing virtually anything disgusting that he managed to do - that exceptional people deserve special concessions. I'm afraid his disease may be spreading.

As I often <u>kiddingly</u> say when I'm talking about building your company's culture and instilling critical values in your people and your business processes: "These are my principles. If you don't like them, I have others." But that's always intended as a joke because – in the real world – we don't get to pick and choose when to honor our promises and commitments. We say what we'll do and then we do what we said we'd do. It couldn't be more straightforward – you don't get to be truthful some of the time or some time later or when it's a better or more convenient time. The truth doesn't vary based on circumstances.

And frankly, I'm not even sure that, in some cases, this is purely an issue of intentional dishonesty or immorality. I think it's just as much a lack of experience and education combined with way too much enthusiasm. Entrepreneurs can talk themselves into anything (I call this the "that hooker really liked me" condition) and, once they do, they want to sell it to the world. But whenever you find that you're having to shade the truth or forget some ugly facts in order to convince yourself or talk your team or some investor into something that you're not even sure you yourself buy off on, you're probably not doing yourself or anyone else a favor. It's almost inevitably a bad deal which you should back away from as quickly as possible.

And, while it's great to be highly motivated, it's not even a little cool if no one trusts your motives. It takes a time and hard work to build any kind of relationship, but just an instant and a suspicion (a long way from proof) to destroy it. And I know just how hard it is to say things that no one wants to hear, but that's part of the leader's job – it's not delegable and it's not optional.

It takes a great deal of experience and a whole bunch of broken dreams and busted relationships to appreciate that to be trusted is a much greater compliment than to be loved. Entrepreneurs – without a doubt – need and want (first and foremost) to be loved. It's part of the sickness which drives us. But, at the end of the day, trust is the only thing that you can really take to the bank.

WHY RABBITS DON'T RUN
BIG BUSINESSES

I've always been partial to Thumper's Dad's advice about communication. In case you don't recall it from the *Bambi* movie, his Dad said: "If you can't say something nice, don't say nothin' at all" - at least as Thumper recalled it. And, as it happens, this is pretty good advice for small talking animals, but it's a really bad way to run your company. You can't build a successful business based on a culture that values quiet, courtesy and consensus over honest conversations, constructive criticism and confrontations where necessary. Politely keeping the peace can't ever trump telling the truth. The best operators know two things for certain: (1) the truth only hurts when you don't tell it and (2) the truth only hurts when it should. I realize that sometimes it's very hard to tell the truth, but it's just as hard to hide it and a whole lot less productive.

White lies and other pleasantries are worthless – they're a lot like eating junk food – you get a temporary lift, but no nourishment; the problem persists; the emptiness returns; and nothing gets done in the meantime. And when you encourage people to lie even a little, you learn quickly that people who will lie for you will eventually lie to you. Better a few bruises and battered egos than a bankrupt business based on bullshitting each other. And honestly, it's just so much easier for everyone because when you always tell the truth, you never have to waste time and energy trying to remember your lies.

Frankly, an aggressive culture where people stand their ground and argue their cases makes for much better ultimate decisions as long as people are arguing for the right reasons. The right reasons are to get to the truth and the best results for the business and not because people need to be right and won't shut up until they grind everyone down and wear everyone else out. Make your point; say your piece; and sit your butt down. Don't argue with the truth.

You want your people to fearlessly face the facts. As one of the great old Hollywood moguls used to say: "I want my people to tell me the truth even if it costs them their jobs". But seriously, unpleasant facts don't fade away when you ignore them – they fester – and refusing to look at them won't change the situation or improve things until you do something about them. Facts may change, but the truth never does. And waiting only makes things worse. It's a funny thing about the truth – the truth doesn't have a time of its own. There's never a better or best time to tell someone the truth – the time for truth is always <u>now</u>.

I think all of the foregoing comes down to a few simple "rules" which you need to share (somewhat obsessively) with all of your people (not just newbies in orientations) on a regular and recurring basis. My suggested and very basic rules are as follows:

(1) <u>Tell the Truth</u>

No shades, no strokes, no "smoothing" the news or softening the blows – give it to me simple and straight. Figures don't lie, but they often don't tell the whole story. Make sure that the metrics don't get in the way of a clear message. As they say, everyone is entitled to their own opinion, but the facts are the facts – you don't get to pick and choose them.

(2) <u>Tell It Timely</u>

Nothing ugly really improves over time. Don't wait to bring me bad news. The sooner and shorter the better. I need a brief, not as book. Nothing elaborate – just accurate information delivered on time and in time.

(3) Tell Everyone

Don't assume that everyone else (or anyone else) necessarily knows what you know. Spread the word. In addition to the general virtues of transparency and making sure that eventually the message does get thru to the right people; going wide makes it more likely that meaningful and actionable information will also get to people who need whether you even realize that or not.

(4) Tell It 'til Someone Listens

I don't think that, in most businesses, you can _ever_ over-communicate relevant and time-sensitive data. But you will often encounter people who fall into two problem piles: (a) people who don't want to say what nobody wants to hear; and (b) people who don't want to hear what needs to and has to be said and spread throughout the organization. These folks are master manipulators and they typically follow the standard three-step routine in dealing with "inconvenient", but sadly true facts: (i) first they aggressively ridicule; (ii) then they violently resist; and finally (iii) they get with the program – claim that they knew it all along – and treat things as obvious and self-evident. You need to keep spreading the word until you're sure that you've done as much as you can reasonably do to let the folks in charge know what you know. If they don't listen after that, so be it. It's frustrating and depressing, but in many businesses, it's a fact of life. As Bruce Springsteen says: "When the truth is spoken and it makes no difference – something in your heart goes cold". After a while, if it's clear that you're wasting your breath, find a better place to be.

(5) Tell It All the Time

And finally, truth-telling is not a sometime thing. As with everything else that matters in your business, it's an everyday, all day part of creating and maintaining an environment where the organization learns and grows and where things continue to improve through a constant iterative process. You can't make innovation through iteration work if you don't have a constant and accurate flow of data telling you what's working and what's not and where you're going wrong.

TELL A SIMPLE STORY

Almost every day I meet and speak with young entrepreneurs trying to get their new businesses off the ground. I don't generally have a lot of time, but I always try to give anyone at least a few minutes to explain what they're trying to do and then I can decide very quickly whether it makes more sense to meet further with them. Frankly, what you can't basically say in ten minutes about your business or your idea really isn't worth saying. I don't think of these little chats as "pitches" (elevator or otherwise) – they're much more like speed dates where you're trying to decide very quickly whether what you're hearing makes sense; whether there's a real business or opportunity lurking there; and whether the person you're speaking to has the passion, enthusiasm and smarts to turn a good idea into a real business.

After 50 years of doing this, I can tell you that it's actually possible to make these initial decisions with a high degree of accuracy in a matter of minutes. Now I admit that I will definitely miss out on a few real opportunities and turn down or not pursue some very talented people, but, by and large – especially since we're all dealing with limited time and scarce resources – the system works and works pretty well.

And here's the main reason why – it's not that I'm so perceptive and smart; it's that way too many people make it too easy to turn them down because they're so unprepared to take their best shot in the moment when the opportunity is there and because they don't really understand how to make the most of that short window of time.

As we used to say in the music industry, it's really easy to tell when a song is bad, but only the public and the market will ultimately decide what sells. Note that I said "what sells", not necessarily what's good. The music business today is all about selling disks and downloads, not making great music. Always has been; always will be.

And it's the same story with describing new businesses. If you're all over the place; if you're trying to be all things to too many people; if your story is so complicated that it's hard to even follow; or if you've got a solution in search of a problem, it's going to be pretty easy to say "thanks, but no thanks". You've got one shot, one moment, and one opportunity to get right to the heart of the matter and the most crucial part of the entire process is to tell a simple story.

How simple? Your story should answer 3 simple questions about your company which, by the way, are the very same questions that will inform and guide your company for its entire existence. These answers are also every bit as significant for each and every employee as they are for any investors. So it's pretty important to get the answers right at the outset. The answers might change over time, but the fundamental questions never do.

Here they are:

Who are We?

Management and team members' <u>relevant</u> experience and credentials

Where are We Going?

Short and long term objectives and goals – abbreviated milestones – timeframe

Why?

What problem is being addressed and solved – time, money, productivity, status

Short, sweet and to the point. You've got to be a ruthless editor and there's no question that the hardest choices are about what to leave out, not what to include. You need to think of both detail and elaboration as forms of pollution. Cut to the quick. And stick to your story.

One of the nastiest things venture guys like to do to "newbies" is to ask them how big their businesses can be and how many opportunities and directions there are to grow the businesses. And when they charge off into the future and start building their castles in the sky; the VCs look at each other, roll their eyes, and say to themselves: "Boy, this guy's not focused at all."

It's an old but important trick from debate class — tell the story you need to tell, be relentless, stay on point, keep it short, and make the limited time that you have count. Everything else can come later. Bottom line: tell a simple story.

BE A ROLE PLAYER OR
ROLL YOUR OWN?

There's a lot of conversation these days about being an entrepreneur and starting your own business and it's very reminiscent of the early dotcom days when everyone thought they'd spend a few dollars, quickly build a website, and just wait for the bucks to start rolling in. Everyone knows how well that worked out for the lion's share of the companies, but many young people today haven't taken the inescapable lessons of those frothy times to heart. They think that starting a business is like learning to swim the hard way – you jump (or a helpful parent or older sibling tosses you) into the deep end of the pool - and everyone (except maybe your older brother) hopes you quickly figure things out and that you don't drown. To put this vignette into the proper perspective, the end of this particular fantasy would be that you'd swim a couple of lengths and then emerge as a slightly better swimmer than Michael Phelps.

In addition, there's another strain of embarrassing arrogance floating around the West Coast where the "Y" guys maintain that they can identify a good, young and talented team of guys with a mediocre idea and then, by magic and the massive application of money, their "expertise", and their network connections, invent a new and better business for the team to build. This is, by and large, utter BS and the few pivots and successful examples that have worked out shouldn't mislead the vast majority of us into thinking that this approach makes the slightest sense. Your idea may change over time and, in many cases, it will have to, but at least it's your idea. If you're plowing someone else's field or chasing another man's dream, at the end of the day, you're just a hired hand. So stick with making your own best ideas real – this startup stuff is just too hard to be doing for someone else. And I get that everyone's dream these days is to be working for themselves building an exciting new business. That's where we'd all like to end up, but that's not where the journey starts.

I spoke recently to a young man who said that he had decided that he really wants to work for a technology startup. I, myself, would like to grow at least 10 inches and play center for the Celtics. I'd say we have about the same long-term prospects because just wanting doesn't make anything so. It's good to have desire, but the details don't take care of themselves. Passion needs to be melded with preparation and planning. A goal without a concrete plan to get there is just a daydream or a delusion. Your plan doesn't have to be the world's greatest anything. It doesn't have to be complete; it doesn't have to be perfect; and it's going to change a million times along the way, but it's a place to start. As we used to say in the movie business, "the screenplay isn't the movie that finally gets made, but it's what gets the movie made."

And, as many times as I have said that an entrepreneur's ignorance can be a competitive advantage in some respects, the truth is that you don't get into this crazy game simply by knocking on a business's front door and asking nicely. If wishes were fishes, every boy would be driving a Porsche. But hope alone is not a strategy for success.

And that's why, when I was asked the question about whether it's better at the outset to be a founder or to work for a startup and learn the ropes, it wasn't even a close question. The odds of achieving some ultimate happiness and financial success are at least 1000% better if you take the time to learn your craft and develop a valuable set of skills in some area that interests you and where you've got some aptitude. After that, the sky really is the only limit.

So plan to be a great employee and to grow into an important role player first and build your future path and your next plan from there instead of from nowhere. Just one note of caution – try to work for someone who can actually teach you something of actual value – not a person who's been doing things the same way forever or someone who's 15 minutes older than you and learning the job as he or she goes. Also it's a really good idea to try to work for someone who has fewer emotional and mental problems than you have.

So that's job number one – get started, start learning, and go from there. Then, and only then, can you start thinking about your next step. Just like Cinderella, if you want to get a great job at a great company, you've got to bring something to the Ball. You'll need the skills you developed in the jobs you've had before (not anything you learned in school) along with a killer work ethic as well as unbelievable persistence. With that kind of package, you're actually worth hiring.

COULD IT BE MAGIC?

I t's National Magic Week. I've been a "professional" magician since I was about 9 years old and I firmly believe that nothing in my training or background (except my mother's raising me to have a level of ridiculous confidence which was utterly disproportionate to my actual looks and abilities) has had a greater impact on my success as an entrepreneur than practicing magic for my peers and their parents. Every prospective entrepreneur should have to learn to perform and "sell" a dozen tricks to an unruly crowd. The lessons learned are good for a lifetime.

Frankly, the kids in the birthday party audience were always easy to control and to fool…the parents (especially those paying me to perform) not so much. They always insisted on seeing how the tricks were done and, as everyone knows, a good magician never tells. Managing the adults and telling them "No" was a learning experience that was at least as valuable as learning how to deal from the bottom of the deck or to pull a sickly little rabbit from a hat.

And the truth is that - as much as people ask you for the explanation or to "tell them the truth" - they actually all prefer the magic of the illusion to knowing how the effect was accomplished. They just don't realize it until it's too late. Because once we know how the trick was done, it loses all its power to amaze, inspire and confound us. No one really wants to see how the sausage was made.

If this is starting to sound a little like an entrepreneur's daily journey; it's not a coincidence. Selling yourself and your team and your investors on your dream every day is itself a magical act. Starting a new business is a triumph of imagination over intelligence and passion over experience. Because – as I always say – if any of us knew how long and hard the actual process was going to be, we probably would never have started down the path in the first place.

Startups have a great deal in common with magic.

First, they involve masterful storytelling. When you look closely at a magician's performance, you realize that the power and the passion is in the dramatic way that the trick is explained and the story is told. The effect (the action) is just a technical process which is more about engineering than emotion. Capturing and conveying that excitement and enthusiasm is what the best entrepreneurs do every day.

Second, they involve the willful suspension of disbelief – at least for a while. We don't believe for a minute that the woman is going to be chopped in half, but we go along with the gag and the guillotine and our hearts race all the same as the blade descends. Setting off to change an industry, invent a new way of doing things, save thousands of lives, etc. isn't something that happens every day, but these things will never happen if we don't believe that they can and try to turn those dreams into realities. Feasibility will compromise us all in the end, but we have to believe in our dreams – however impossible they may seem – and never let the turkeys get us down.

And finally, we are blessed to be living in an age of amazing new technologies available to millions of people across the world. The truth is that any sufficiently advanced technology is basically indistinguishable from magic anyway. If we continue to create and capture the multitude of opportunities out there today to combine our vibrant imaginations with our powerful new technologies, we can all be magicians in our own right. If you can dream it, you can do it. Because, as they say at Disney, the magic's the magic within you.

ABOUT THE AUTHOR

Howard Tullman is the CEO of 1871 in Chicago where digital startups get their start. He is also the General Managing Partner of two venture funds: Chicago High- Tech Investment Partners and G2T3V, LLC, which both focus on funding disruptive innovators. He is the former Chairman and CEO of Tribeca Flashpoint Media Arts Academy in Chicago. He is an active member of numerous city, state and civic boards and organizations and a tireless supporter and mentor to many start-ups and other businesses and individuals. He has successfully founded more than a dozen high-tech businesses in his 50 year career and created more than $1 billion in investor value as well as thousands of new jobs. He writes a regular weekly blog on The Perspiration Principles for Inc. Magazine and can be directly contacted:

- by email at h@1871.com
- on twitter @tullman
- his blog: tullman.blogspot.com
- his primary website: www.tullman.com

To get all of Howard's blog posts in one download, visit Blogintobook.com/tullman/.